Illuminate
Publishing

WJEC

AS Sociology

Study and Revision Guide

David Bown

•

Janis Griffiths

•

Barbara Greenall

Published in 2011 by Illuminate Publishing Ltd, P.O Box 1160, Cheltenham, Gloucestershire GL50 9RW

Orders: Please visit www.illuminatepublishing.com
or email sales@illuminatepublishing.com

British Library Cataloguing in Publication Data

A catalogue record for this book is available from the British Library

ISBN 978-0-9568401-0-3

Printed and bound in Great Britain by 4edge Ltd, Hockley.

The publisher's policy is to use papers that are natural, renewable and recyclable products made from wood grown in sustainable forests. The logging and manufacturing processes are expected to conform to the environmental regulations of the country of origin.

Every effort has been made to contact copyright holders of material reproduced in this book. If notified, the publishers will be pleased to rectify any errors or omissions at the earliest opportunity.

Editor: Geoff Tuttle

Cover design: Nigel Harriss

Text design and layout: Nigel Harriss

Permissions

All images ©Shutterstock. Individual credits as follows: p07 Andrejs Pidjass; p07 gillmar; p11 Losevsky Pavel; p12 Yuri Arcurs ; p18 DFree; p20 MNStudio; p21 Losevsky Pavel; p22 ANdresr; p24 kentoh; p25 Pixel Memoirs; p26 Monkey Business Images; p27 wavebreakmedia ltd ; p31 modernlove ; p32 wet nose; p34 Gordon Swanson; p36 LesPaleni; p36 Sergey Chirkov; p37 bikeriderlondon; p38 Monkey Business Images; p39 Dmitriy Shironosov; p41 Maria Bell; p43 Iurii Konoval; p49 wrangler; p52 Chad McDermott; p60 Ewa Walicka ; p62 Bianda Ahmad Hisham; p63 jennyt; p65 Maridav; p66 R. Gino Santa Maria; p67 Viorel Sima; p68 Pres Panayotov; p70 Nicemonkey; p79 J. Henning Buchholz; p81 1809056 Ontario Ltd.

Acknowledgements

We are very grateful to the team at Illuminate Publishing for their professionalism, support and guidance throughout this project. Without their help, we would not have undertaken or completed this book. It has been a pleasure to work so closely with them.

The authors and publisher wish to thank Joanna Lewis and Steve James of WJEC for their support and enthusiasm for this book.

Dedication

To Mary, my love, rock and inspiration. DB

For my family, who are everything to me. JG

To all of the hard working teachers whose efforts make so much impact on the future life chances of their students. BG

Browns
BS 1426574
19/8/13

£12-99

Contents

How to use this book

The contents of this study and revision guide are designed to guide you through to success in the WJEC Sociology AS level examination. It has been written by the senior examining team for the WJEC specification so that you will be aware of what is required.

There are notes for the compulsory sections of each examination:

SY1 – The Compulsory Core

SY2 – Research Methods

In addition, there are detailed notes for the two most popular options from each examination paper:

SY1 – Family and Youth Culture

SY2 – Education and Mass Media

You will probably only study one option for each examination paper in any depth, but will benefit from developing your wider knowledge by looking at the alternative options as well.

Knowledge and understanding

The **first section** of the book covers the key knowledge required for the examination. Here you will find summary notes of the important debates.

In addition, we have tried to give you additional pointers so that you can develop your work:

- Any of the terms in the WJEC specification can be used as the basis of a question, so we have highlighted those terms and offered definitions. You could use these notes as the basis of revision cards.

- There are Quickfire questions designed to test your knowledge and understanding of the material.

- We have offered examination advice based on experience of what candidates need to do attain the highest grades.

- We have also highlighted key figures and research so that you are reminded of the importance of referring to writers and evidence when writing your answers.

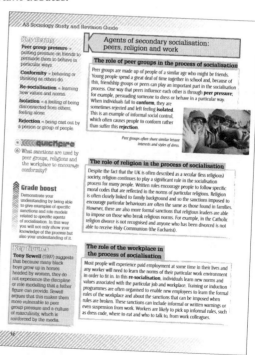

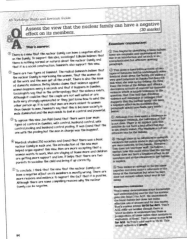

Exam practice and technique

The **second section** of the book covers the key skills for examination success and offers you examples based on real-life responses to examination commands. First you will be guided into an understanding of how the examination system works, and then offered clues to success.

After that, there are a variety of sample answers to possible questions in the options. These are not model answers and you should not attempt to learn them. They offer a guide as to the standard that is required, and the commentary will explain why the responses gained the marks that they did. You will be offered advice on how to tailor your writing to produce an effective piece of extended writing.

Most importantly, we advise that you should take responsibility for your own learning and not rely on your teachers to give you notes or tell you how to gain the grades that you require. You should look for additional notes to support your study into WJEC Sociology.

We advise that you look at the WJEC website www.wjec.co.uk. In particular, you need to be aware of the specification. Look for specimen examination papers and mark schemes. You may find past papers useful as well.

In addition, look at the website of the NGfL Cymru www.ngfl-cymru. org.uk/vtc-home/vtc-post-16-home/vtc-as_sociology.htm for a range of supplementary material written by teachers of the WJEC Sociology specification.

Good luck with your revision.

David Bown

Janis Griffiths

Barbara Greenall

Knowledge and Understanding

SY1 The Compulsory Core

The SY1 examination is concerned with how individuals become part of society and how they learn social rules. The compulsory core is focussed on culture, social control and way that we become human through our contact with others. The core examines how institutions pass on norms and values. Questions are likely to focus on testing knowledge and understanding of the process of acquiring culture. A sound understanding of primary and secondary socialisation is essential.

Revision checklist

Tick column 1 when you have completed brief revision notes.
Tick column 2 when you think you have a good grasp of the topic.
Tick column 3 during final revision when you feel you have mastery of the topic.

			1	2	3
p7	**What is culture and why is it so important to Sociology?**	Cultural diversity			
		Subcultures			
p8	**What is socialisation?**	Why is socialisation important?			
		Feral children			
p9	**How are people socialised?**	Primary socialisation			
		Secondary socialisation			
		Agents of socialisation			
		The role of the family in socialisation			
p10	**Agents of secondary socialisation: education**	The role of education in the process of socialisation			
		The formal curriculum			
		Formal social control			
		The informal curriculum			
		Informal social control			
p11	**Agents of secondary socialisation: media**	The role of the media in the process of socialisation			
p12	**Agents of secondary socialisation: peers, religion and work**	The role of peer groups in the process of socialisation			
		The role of religion in the process of socialisation			
		The role of the workplace in the process of socialisation			

What is culture and why is it so important to sociology?

What do these babies know about culture?

In simple terms **culture** means the values, norms, meanings beliefs and customs of any society. It is a word that describes a way of life. Sociologists are interested in culture because it separates humans from wild creatures; in short culture makes us human.

Humans need to learn how to behave, they are not born knowing how to walk, how to eat, how to use a toilet or how to speak. These skills are learned but the precise nature of the skills can vary from one society to another. For example, in China it is customary to eat with chopsticks, whereas in Britain it is customary to eat with a knife and fork; such cultural skills are learned.

Cultural diversity

Diversity simply means difference and there are numerous examples of different cultures around the world. Cultural identity and cultural difference can be demonstrated through language, clothing or symbols and these characteristics of culture are often most evident in National events such as the Olympics or the Football or Rugby World Cups. At such events cultural symbols, such as flags and national dress, are often evident as a sign of shared identity. Some cultures have values and norms that are very different to the ones with which we are familiar. These differences often make other cultures seem strange, but this is merely because their norms and values are unfamiliar to us. In a study of the Tchambuli people of New Guinea, for example, Margaret Mead found that women shave their heads and wear no jewellery, whilst men wear ornaments, and curl their hair. Culture is therefore said to be **socially constructed**, that is, made by society and the people in it and it is passed on from one generation to the next through the process of socialisation.

Subcultures

In **multi-cultural** Britain there are many examples of **subcultures** with their own particular values and norms that give them a distinctive character.

How does this American Indian demonstrate his culture?

Key Terms

Culture = the values, norms and customs of a society.

Subculture = a culture within a culture with some different values and norms such as ways of dressing.

Multi-cultural = a society in which there are a number of different cultures often linked to ethnicity.

Socially constructed = made by society.

quickfire

① Why are sociologists interested in culture?

Grade boost

Make sure that you are able to give examples of the component parts of culture such as values, norms, symbols and customs.

Key Terms

Feral = wild.

Unsocialised = someone who has not been socialised into the culture of their society.

Socialisation = the process of learning culture.

quickfire

② What evidence or examples could be used to show that socialisation is important to humans?

Grade boost

Remember that socialisation is fundamental to the acquisition of culture.

What is socialisation?

The term **socialisation** refers to the process of learning the culture of any given society. When an individual has not learned the norms and values of the society in which they live, they are often referred to as **unsocialised**.

Why is socialisation important?

Functionalists regard the process of socialisation as an essential part of the establishment of social order and social equilibrium. They maintain that socialisation is vital for the well-being of individuals and for society as a whole because it enables people to 'fit in'. Marxists, on the other hand, claim that the ruling class control socialisation and pass on their values and norms, which enables them to control the subject class, which Althusser calls ideological control.

Feral children

Unsocialised children are usually referred to as **feral** (wild) children. Although it is not common to find children who have had little or no contact with humans, there are some famous examples and they offer compelling evidence of the importance of socialisation for humans. In the late 1980s, for example, newspapers told the world about 'puppy boy', Horst, so named because his parents left him in the care of the pet Alsatian while they went out drinking. Horst copied the dog's behaviour; he whimpered like a dog, crawled like a dog, slept curled up like a dog and ate raw chicken. Horst behaved just like Asta, the dog who had taken care of him. Another famous example is that of Genie, a girl discovered at the age of 13 after being locked away by her father for 11 years. Genie had not learned how to walk, talk, eat, or to use a toilet, because she has been deprived of human contact.

So it is clear that the early years of a child's life are very significant in the acquisition of culture. In these early years children learn, through socialisation, how to fit into the society into which they are born, in short, they learn how to be human.

How are people socialised?

Socialisation is a lifelong process but it is generally divided into two stages: **primary socialisation** and **secondary socialisation**.

Primary socialisation

Primary socialisation is the first stage in the process of learning about culture. It occurs in the early years of life through contact with family members, carers and other children. It can also include contact with the media or media products.

Secondary socialisation

This is the second stage of the socialisation process, which occurs after the period of early childhood and continues throughout life. It involves contact with a number of different institutions and individuals such as schools, work, peer group and the media.

Agents of socialisation

This is the name given to the institutions involved in transmitting the norms and values of society through the process of socialisation; for example, family, schools, peers, the media, religion and work.

The role of the family in socialisation

In their early years, children learn norms, values and rules for living as well as how they are expected to behave as males and females. What children learn can vary according to social class, ethnicity, religion and locale. However, how these things are learned, in other words the process of socialisation, is likely to be similar in many families. For example, families may use sanctions. **Sanctions** are reactions to behaviour designed to either reinforce the behaviour or to stop it from happening again. Positive sanctions usually involve praise. For example, if a young child says please and thank you, a parent might praise them for being well-mannered. Negative sanctions, on the other hand, may involve a punishment such as the 'naughty step' or depriving the child of something that they like.

Ann Oakley claims that children learn gender roles within the family through **canalisation** and **manipulation**. Through manipulation a parent may pay attention to a girl's hair and appearance and so she learns that these are important to her identity as a female. Canalisation directs boys and girls towards rehearsing their adult roles through role play using different sorts of toys such as dolls and miniature cookers for girls and construction toys and guns for boys.

Key Terms

Primary socialisation = the first stage in the process of learning about culture.

Secondary socialisation = the second stage in the process of learning about culture.

Role models = people who are admired and imitated.

Imitation = copying behaviour.

Sanction = reactions to behaviour.

Canalisation = channelling a child's activities in relation to their gender.

Manipulation = persuading a child to think about themselves in particular ways in relation to their gender.

quickfire

③ What is the difference between what we learn and how we learn it?

Key figure

Ann Oakley wrote about the ways in which families socialise children into their gender roles through specific strategies.

Grade boost

It is important to be able to explain how children learn the norms and values of their culture and to be able to offer appropriate examples to illustrate this.

Key Terms

Formal social control
= control through written rules.

Informal social control = control through unwritten rules.

Formal curriculum = the subjects taught in schools.

Informal curriculum = norms and values learned in school.

Ethnocentric = the belief that one culture is superior to others.

quickfire

④ What is the difference between formal and informal social control? Is social control different to socialisation?

Grade boost

It is important to be able to offer examples of formal and informal social control and in this way demonstrate an understanding of the difference between the ways in which we learn about culture through the agents of socialisation.

Key figures

John Abraham (1995) In his research in a comprehensive school Abraham concluded that there was evidence of gender stereotyping in textbooks.

Agents of secondary socialisation: education

The role of education in the process of socialisation

Schools are one of the agents of secondary socialisation and they employ both informal and formal ways of controlling behaviour and transmitting society's norms and values.

The formal curriculum

The **formal curriculum** includes the subjects taught in schools and the content of lessons. The formal curriculum is controlled up to Key Stage 4 (Year 10) by the National Curriculum decided by the government and it includes knowledge that is seen to be important. Not everyone agrees that what children are taught in the National Curriculum is essential to their knowledge. The formal curriculum has been criticised by writers such as Gillborn for being **ethnocentric**, that is focused on one ethnicity.

Formal social control

Schools can control children formally through written school rules. When these rules are broken, formal sanctions are employed to discourage a repeat of the behaviour, such as report cards, letters home or detention. Praise is another sanction designed to encourage a repeat of the behaviour and this can take the form of praise assemblies, merit marks and special privileges.

The informal curriculum

The **informal** or hidden curriculum is said to play a very significant role in the socialisation of pupils. Pupils absorb norms and values without realising they are doing so. They may imitate adult role models such as teachers or even older pupils and learn important messages about expected behaviour and about gender by watching how males and females behave. Despite changing attitudes amongst females Sue Lees' 1986 research concluded that many girls experienced stereotypical socialisation that influenced their future expectations. Similarly, Abraham's 1995 research concluded that in maths textbooks males were likely to be represented in active roles whilst women were often portrayed buying food or using washing machines. It is through this subliminal socialisation and role modelling that males and females may establish part of their gender identity.

Informal social control

Behaviour can be controlled informally through the demonstration of disappointment, pleasure and even facial expressions. Teachers and fellow students (peers) are involved in this process.

Agents of secondary socialisation: media

The role of the media in the process of socialisation

We are said to live in a media-saturated society and as a result the media in all of its many forms has an increasingly significant influence in secondary socialisation. The media can be television, film, music, newspapers, magazines, the Internet and indeed anything that sends messages to a large and widespread audience.

The way in which people are socialised by the media is more focused on role models and imitation than on the imposition of sanctions. Content analysis of the media often reveals persistently stereotypical images and messages, and this has been particularly true of those associated with gender. For example, boys might aspire to be like their sporting hero or to follow the latest fashion craze. Similarly, girls might be persuaded that a particular size or body shape is ideal simply because of the images and messages about size and style that they see in a range of media products. Marjorie Ferguson's 1983 research supports what McRobbie found in the 1970s, claiming that women's magazines convey what Ferguson calls a 'cult of femininity'. Rutherford also refers to media messages about gender; he suggests that male identity is changing. There has been increased interest in male cosmetics and toiletries, which, according to Rutherford is because of targeted media advertising and role modelling.

The media has also been linked with juvenile crime and so-called 'copycat violence', with the suggestion that individuals watch and then imitate what they see. The use of social networking sites such as Facebook along with technological advances in the ways that mobile phones can be used have opened up new ways for the media to influence and shape people's everyday lives. So the media can be a source of information about gender, style, knowledge and identity, and through imitation individuals are socialised into the norms and values of the society in which they live.

Key Term

Consumer culture = a culture which places great importance on buying goods and services.

quickfire

⑤ What are subliminal messages and why might they be important?

Grade boost

It is important to be able to offer good examples of how the media can influence people.

Key figures

Marjorie Ferguson (1983) found in her study of young women's magazines that they promoted a traditional idea of femininity. She also suggested that these magazines encouraged females to aspire to traditional roles of wife and mother, and home making rather than career.

New technologies extend the ways that the media can socialise us.

quickfire

⑥ What sanctions are used by peer groups, religions and the workplace to encourage conformity?

Grade boost

Demonstrate your understanding by being able to give examples of specific sanctions and role models related to specific agents of socialisation. In this way you will not only show your knowledge of the process but also your understanding of it.

Key figures

Tony Sewell (1997) suggests that because many black boys grow up in homes headed by women, they do not experience the discipline or role modelling that a father figure can provide. Sewell argues that this makes them more vulnerable to peer group pressure and a culture of masculinity, which is reinforced by the media.

Agents of secondary socialisation: peers, religion and work

The role of peer groups in the process of socialisation

Peer groups are made up of people of a similar age who might be friends. Young people spend a great deal of time together in school and, because of this, friendship groups or peers can play an important part in the socialisation process. One way that peers influence each other is through **peer pressure**; for example, persuading someone to dress or behave in a particular way. When individuals fail to **conform**, they are sometimes rejected and left feeling **isolated**. This is an example of informal social control, which often causes people to conform rather than suffer this **rejection**.

Peer groups often share similar leisure interests and styles of dress.

The role of religion in the process of socialisation

Despite the fact that the UK is often described as a secular (less religious) society, religion continues to play a significant role in the socialisation process for many people. Written rules encourage people to follow specific moral codes that are reflected in the norms of particular religions. Religion is often closely linked to family background and so the sanctions imposed to encourage particular behaviours are often the same as those found in families. However, there are also more formal sanctions that religious leaders are able to impose on those who break religious norms. For example, in the Catholic religion divorce is not recognised and anyone who has been divorced is not able to receive Holy Communion (the Eucharist).

The role of the workplace in the process of socialisation

Most people will experience paid employment at some time in their lives and any worker will need to learn the norms of their particular work environment in order to fit in. In this **re-socialisation**, individuals learn new norms and values associated with the particular job and workplace. Training or induction programmes are often organised to enable new employees to learn the formal rules of the workplace and about the sanctions that can be imposed when rules are broken. These sanctions can include informal or written warnings or even suspension from work. Workers are likely to pick up informal rules, such as dress code, where to eat and who to talk to, from work colleagues.

The Compulsory Core: Summary

What is Sociology?

It is important to understand that at the heart of Sociology is the fundamental question, why is society like it is and why do we behave as we do?

What is culture and why is it important?

Culture is the way of life of a society. It describes how people in society understand their world. It bonds people in common understandings and shared patterns of behaviour. It is of great interest to the Sociologist as it forms the basis of society.

Where does culture come?

Culture can come from individuals or from powerful groups who impose their will on others. The study of culture helps us to realise that Sociology provides us with a range of perspectives that we can use to discuss the answers to questions.

How do we acquire (learn) culture?

Being human is more than a biological categorisation; it involves learning how to fit in to the society into which you are born. So we learn culture through our contact with others.

What are agents of socialisation and why are they important?

These are the groups and institutions that pass on culture and they play a very important part in the process of 'fitting in'. These agents use social control in the form of sanctions and role modelling to pass on norms and values and control behaviour.

Why is it important to understand how culture is passed on?

If we understand how culture is passed on, we can better understand the ways in which our behaviour can be controlled and our values and norms are shaped. Understanding and being able to discuss this process is at the core of Sociology.

SY1 Families and Culture

The SY1 examination is concerned with how individuals become part of society and how social rules are made. The family, in whatever form, plays an important part in this process. Families are usually the most important agency of primary socialisation for babies and children. Families are important in terms of our relationships with significant others such as partners, siblings, parents and children. A family can be a safe haven from a cruel world or a secret place where violence and abuse take place. Questions will tend to focus on topical debates about the role of the family and on discussions about the impact of demographic change.

Revision checklist

Tick column 1 when you have completed brief revision notes.
Tick column 2 when you think you have a good grasp of the topic.
Tick column 3 during final revision when you feel you have mastery of the topic.

			1	2	3
p16	**Family key terms and topical debates**	What does the term family mean?			
		What is the most dominant definition of family?			
p17	**Family structures in contemporary society**	Traditional nuclear family			
		Extended families			
		Reconstituted (blended) families			
p18	**Diversity of family structures**	Inter-ethnic families			
		Lone parent families			
		Same sex families			
p19	**Demographic change: patterns and trends**	How have divorce rates changed?			
		Why has there been an increase in divorce?			
p20	**Demographic change: marriage rates**	How have marriage rates changed?			
		What are the reasons for these changes?			
		Other key trends			
p21	**Demographic change: birth and mortality rates**	How have birth rates changed?			
		What are the reasons for these changes?			
		How have mortality rates changed?			
		What are the reasons for these changes and what impact might they have?			

Family key terms and topical debates

Key Terms

Kinship = ties through blood or marriage.

Heterosexual = attracted to members of the opposite sex.

Breadwinner = traditional male role of primary wage earner for the family.

Cohabitation = living together as man and wife without being married.

Grade boost

Understand that the definition of the term family has important implications for the way we live and for government policy. Try to show that you understand this in your essays.

quickfire

① Why is it difficult to decide on a simple definition of the term family in contemporary society?

Key figures

Allan and Crow suggest that definitions of family have been made more complicated by changing patterns of divorce, remarriage and cohabitation.

What does the term family mean?

The term family is frequently used but its precise meaning is not necessarily agreed upon by everyone. For example, a family might include partners and their children but it might also include other relatives. It is generally agreed that **kinship** is an important part of what we mean by family. Kinship means ties through blood or marriage. However, individuals with no blood or marriage ties are sometimes given honorary titles such as aunt or uncle to indicate their close emotional bond with the family. The meaning of family is further complicated by changing patterns of marriage, divorce, remarriage and **cohabitation**. So there is no single definition of family, indeed the increasingly diverse nature of family forms means that the meaning of family is becoming more complex.

Postmodernists suggest that it is better to use the term families because this allows for a number of different interpretations of the term. The precise meaning of the term family is significant because the way that it is defined has implications for government policy relating to the family and family life.

What is the most dominant definition of family?

Functionalist ideas about the family have been very influential in defining what is meant by family. The traditional nuclear family containing a mother, father and their biological children has been the most commonly used definition of the term family. This nuclear family is based on a **heterosexual** relationship between the adult partners who are romantically in love. In this family the female is more involved in housework and child care and the male is the main **breadwinner**. This traditional definition of what a family means has shaped our thinking about family life and is referred to as family ideology. Family ideology has an important influence on social policy, such as the lack of provision of free child care, which could stem from the belief that child care is the responsibility of mothers.

Family structures in contemporary society

Traditional nuclear family

The traditional nuclear family could mean a heterosexual married couple living with their biological children. It could also include Murdock's idea that the children can be biological or adopted; either way, it is evident that the nuclear family remains very much a part of contemporary society. Research studies show that many people regard this type of family structure as the most desirable one even though nuclear families are in the minority in terms of household types. Nevertheless, it is likely that significant numbers of people will experience life in a nuclear family at some stage in their lives.

Extended families

Extended families can be either **vertically extended** or **horizontally extended**. Vertically extended families, which are sometimes referred to as beanpole families, consist of three or more generations who live together or close by. This type of family structure is becoming more common as young people are forced, because of financial constraints, to live longer with parents and because elderly grandparents may move in with their children.

Horizontally extended families consist of relatives from two generations who live together or near to one another, for example the wife's brothers or sisters and their children. The modified extended family is another variation on the extended type. Modified extended families consist of extended kin who do not live close to one another but who have regular contact either in person or with the help of communication technology.

Janet Foster's research in the late 1990s suggests that extended families are an important source of support, and data from a 2003 ONS survey revealed that extended family ties are often maintained through technology such as email.

Reconstituted (blended) families

Reconstituted (blended) families are sometimes known as stepfamilies and they are an increasingly common family type. They consist of one or both partners who have children from a previous relationship living with them. This type of family might be the result of divorce. It is very common, following a divorce, for children to remain with their mother, meaning that stepfathers are a common feature of reconstituted families. The new couple may go on to have their own biological children who become stepbrothers or sisters to their siblings.

Key Terms

Vertically extended family = a family with three or more generations living together or close by.

Horizontally extended family = a family with two generations and wider kin such as uncles, aunts and cousins.

Reconstituted (blended) family = a family consisting of one or more previous families.

Grade boost

Make sure that you know what types of family structure exist in contemporary society and the implications of this.

quickfire

② Why are there more reconstituted families in contemporary society?

Key figure

Bernades claims that contemporary families are so diverse that there is no simple definition of family. He suggests that it is better to use the term families rather than family as this embraces the concept of diversity.

Key Terms

Conjugal relationship = the relationship between two adult partners either married or cohabiting.

Egalitarian = equal.

Delinquent = behaving in an antisocial or illegal way.

Heterosexual = attracted to people from the opposite sex.

Homosexual = attracted to people from the same sex.

Grade boost

It is important to know about the structural diversity of family forms and the reasons for this diversity as well as the ways in which this diversity affects the lived experiences of individuals.

quickfire

③ What is meant by the ideology of the family and why are Sociologists interested in this concept?

Key figures

Barrett and McIntosh claim that the notion that the nuclear family is the 'best' type of family devalues other ways of living and this makes people who do choose to live in a different way feel marginalised.

Sir Elton John and his partner David Furnish have recently celebrated the birth of a son born to a surrogate mother.

Diversity of family structures

Inter-ethnic families

Inter-ethnic families include partners who come from different ethnic backgrounds. Berthoud (2000) found that British born individuals of African-Caribbean origin were more likely than any other group to intermarry. Only one quarter of African-Caribbean children live with two Black parents. Children born to parents from different ethnic backgrounds are referred to as mixed race and they often face unique problems linked to racial prejudice and discrimination. The number of children who are of mixed race has increased significantly over recent years. The 2001 census introduced a new category of 'mixed race' in order to collect information form this growing group of people.

Lone parent families

Lone parent families, as the name suggests, are ones in which there is only one parent. This type of family makes up approximately 25% of all families. Of these lone parent families 90% are headed by women, who may be divorcees, separated, widowed or never married women, or women who have chosen singlehood. New Right thinkers claim that lone parent families are the source of many social problems especially those associated with **delinquent** young males. They also claim that too much State support in the form of benefits is given to single parents. These negative views of single parent families are strongly criticised by Feminists, in particular, who claim that any social problems associated with children from single parent families are more likely to be linked with poverty than with the lack of a male role model.

Same sex families

Cultural tolerance of family diversity is exemplified by the wider acceptance of same sex families. The State has recognised this type of partnership by making Civil Partnerships available to same sex couples through the Civil Partnerships Act of 2004, which allowed same sex couples to publicly declare their commitment in a marriage style ceremony. Weekes *et al.* (1997) suggest

that same sex families are based on choice and the negotiation of roles and expectations. Because of this, **conjugal relationship**s in same sex couples are often more **egalitarian** than those found in **heterosexual** relationships.

Demographic change: patterns and trends

Key Terms

Secularisation = decline in the importance of religion.

Stigmatised = regarded as shameful.

Normalised = regarded as normal.

How have divorce rates changed?

In comparison to other European countries the divorce rate in Britain is high. It increased dramatically in 1970 and 1993 and, despite falling slightly towards the end of the 1990s, it rose again in 2002. Of those divorcing in 2005 20 per cent had been divorced before and it is now estimated that 40 per cent of marriages will end in divorce.

Grade boost

Make sure that you understand that there are a range of reasons for the changes in the rate of divorce.

Why has there been an increase in divorce?

- **Changes in the law**
  One of the most obvious reasons for the increase in divorce since 1970 is the change in divorce laws. The 1969 *Divorce Law Reform Act* made it possible to petition for divorce on the grounds that the marriage had irretrievably broken down. No longer did a guilty party need to be found, and making it easier to find the grounds for divorce may well be the reason for the significant increase in divorce in 1970. Similarly, the 1984 *Matrimonial Proceedings Act* reduced the time couples had to be married before seeking a divorce from three years to one year.

- **Cost**
  Reductions in the costs associated with divorce have made it more accessible.

- **The economic independence of women**
  Many women are in paid employment and, even though it is true that women on average earn less than men, their earning power has reduced their dependence on men. This has enabled many women to leave the marital home and petition for divorce.

- **Secularisation**
  The decline in the importance of religion may also have had an impact on divorce rates as may wider cultural changes. As more people get divorced, it is less **stigmatised** and more **normalised**. As fewer people follow a specific religion, there is less opposition to the concept of divorce.

- **Higher expectations of marriage**
  People are less likely to marry for economic reasons in contemporary society and so their expectations of marriage increase. Allan and Crow (2001) suggest that the focus of marriage is now on the relationship and on high expectations of fulfilment and happiness. When these expectations are not realised, the couple may decide to end the marriage and try again with a different partner.

quickfire

④ Why do New Right thinkers regard rising divorce rates as a sign of family decline? Are they correct?

Key figures

Finch and Mason claim that divorce does not always cut the bonds between family members and that these ongoing relationships are evidence of the importance of biological parenthood.

Key Terms

Cohabitation = living as if married without being married.

Genderquake = changing attitudes and aspirations of females.

Singlehood = living alone out of choice.

Surrogate mother = a woman who carries a baby for another person or couple.

Grade boost

Make connections between these patterns and trends and changing family structures and relationships.

quickfire

⑤ Why are Sociologists interested in demographic change?

Key figure

Allan and Crow (2001) suggest that expectations of marriage have changed and that the focus is now on emotional fulfilment. The increased economic independence of women has enabled them to more easily leave a relationship where this fulfilment has not been achieved.

Demographic change: marriage rates

How have marriage rates changed?

Fewer people are choosing to marry in contemporary society and the rate for first-time marriages is declining. There has been a significant growth in **cohabitation** and even when people marry they are marrying at a later age. In 1973 two-thirds of British women in their late twenties were married with children but this had dropped to one-third in the late 1990s. Patricia Morgan, a New Right thinker, regards this decline in marriage rates as a worrying indicator of the state of family life in Britain. This view is contested by Feminists and Postmodernists. It is interesting to note that second and subsequent marriage rates have increased.

What are the reasons for these changes?

- Many people delay marriage but most will marry at some point. The average age for first-time marriage for women is now 29 and for men it is 31.
- Many marriages are remarriages, demonstrating that the value of marriage remains a feature of British culture.
- The changing roles and attitudes of women which Wilkinson (1994) refers to as '**genderquake**' mean that women no longer prioritise marriage and children as they might have done in the past.
- Many people choose to cohabit, using this as a kind of 'trial run' for marriage and this either delays or terminates any marriage plans.
- Relationships are less focussed on economic considerations and more on romantic love. Allan and Crow (2001) suggest that couples have higher expectations of marriage today than they might have had in the past.

Other key trends

There has been a growth in cohabitation and in single-person households. A significant number of people are choosing **singlehood** as a lifestyle choice. This may also be linked to changing employment patterns, which can require individuals to move geographically in search of work. There has also been an increase in the number of same sex couples who not only live together but also have children, for example Elton John and his partner recently announced the birth of their first child born to a **surrogate mother**.

Traditional first-time marriages have become less common in contemporary society.

Demographic change: birth and mortality rates

How have birth rates changed?

Despite remaining fairly constant for many years, in recent years the birth rate declined slightly, and in 2009 stood at 1.94 children per woman in the UK. However, the patterns of fertility are what most interest the Sociologist. For example, women are now having their children much later in life. In 2009 the average age for a woman to have her first child was 29.4 compared to 28.4 ten years earlier. The **fertility rate** for women aged 35+ has increased, though it has decreased for women in their 20s. Hantrais (2006) points out that women in contemporary society are more likely to have their first child as they approach the age of 30.

What are the reasons for these changes?

- Women are more able to control their fertility through birth control or interventions such as the morning after pill or abortion.
- Women may choose to establish their careers before having children.
- Changing attitudes have made it easier for women and couples to remain childless if they so wish.
- Women are having their children in a smaller time span and this is likely to reduce the number of children they have.
- The increasing cost of children may result in couples deciding to remain childless or to limit the size of their family. Children have become an economic liability rather than an economic asset.

How have mortality rates changed?

Mortality rates, or death rates as they are often known, have declined in recent years as people live longer. Life expectancy has increased.

What are the reasons for these changes and what impact might they have?

- Improvements in health care have increased the life expectancy of both males and females.
- Relationships between grandparents and grandchildren may change as they may become more involved with child care.
- Relationships and responsibilities between parents and children may change as the health of ageing parents deteriorates.
- The latter years of life may be characterised by ill health and the increasing likelihood of Alzheimer's disease and a variety of cancers.

Grandparent–grandchild relationships are often very important in family life.

Key Terms

Mortality rate = the number of people dying per thousand population.

Fertility rate = the number of live births per thousand population.

Grade boost

Be aware that more women are having children outside of marriage but not necessarily outside of a stable relationship.

quickfire

⑥ What problems might be created by an ageing population?

Key figure

Charles *et al.* (2008) found in their Swansea-based research that grandparents were regularly involved in caring for their grandchildren, and adult children were involved in caring for their parents. Indeed, older grandchildren were also sometimes involved in caring for their grandparents.

Key Term

Equilibrium = balance.

Grade boost

Use different theories of family as the framework for discussions about whether the nuclear family is the ideal type.

quickfire

⑦ What criticisms can you make of the Functionalist view of the role of the family?

Key figure

Dennis and Erdos claim that where nuclear families have broken down, young males in particular are badly affected. They claim that the absence of a male role model results in them being poorly socialised and unaware of the responsibilities of being a husband and father.

Functionalists and the New Right claim that nuclear family structures are good for society and for individuals.

Sociological debates and theories: Functionalist and New Right ideas about the family

What do Functionalists say about the role of the family in contemporary society?

Functionalists believe that society works in a similar way to the way that a living organism works. There are many systems in a living organism, just as there are many systems in society. In a living organism such as the human body, for example, the heart is essential to the well-being of the body, and its role is to pump blood around the circulatory system. In society, according to Functionalists there are also systems with specific jobs such as the family. Functionalists claim that we have families because they perform essential functions for the well-being of society as a whole. Talcott Parsons suggests that the nuclear family performs two 'basic and irreducible' functions which are:

- **The primary socialisation of children**
  Families pass on society's norms and values so that children can fit into their culture, which helps to maintain social order and **equilibrium**.

- **The stabilisation of adult personalities**
  Partners support each other emotionally and this helps them to remain well-balanced and productive members of society. Family life provides emotional security, comfort and support to family members. This picture of family life is often referred to as 'the warm bath theory', which means that Functionalists give an impression of family life as being like a warm bath soothing everyone and washing away the stress and strain of everyday life.

The New Right

Like Functionalists, the New Right take the view that families are essential for individuals and for society. They go so far as to say that the nuclear family is the best family structure. The New Right are concerned that the family is in decline because of rising divorce, cohabitation, fatherless families and the increase in same sex couples. They claim that social problems, particularly those associated with young boys can be traced to the lack of a male role model.

In short, Functionalists and the New Right believe that nuclear families are essential for individuals and for society and other family types should be discouraged.

Sociological debates and theories: Marxist ideas about the family

Key Terms

Internalised = learning something so that it becomes part of an individual's normal way of thinking.

Ideological control = controlling what a person or group of people think.

Status quo = the existing situation or state of affairs.

Exploitation = taking advantage of a person or group of people.

What do Marxists say about the role of the family?

Marxists claim that society is like a large system of interconnecting parts. However, unlike Functionalists, Marxists claim that all of these parts are controlled by the ruling class (bourgeoisie) who use their power to ensure that ruling class ideas are passed on and **internalised** by the subject class (proletariat). In this way the ruling class are able to achieve **ideological control**. Marx believed that in capitalist economies, institutions such as the family exist to serve the needs of the capitalist system. For example, capitalism is based on producing and selling goods for profit. Workers (the proletariat) can only offer their labour in return for wages. These wages are kept low so that profits can stay high for the owners (bourgeoisie). In turn, workers are persuaded through advertising to use their wages to buy the goods that they have helped to make. Zaretsky (1976) claimed that by performing household tasks and socialising the next generation of workers, women were helping to maintain capitalism. Controversially, Engels suggests that families and marriage are an invention of men who owned private property that they wished to be passed on to their natural offspring.

According to Marxists, the family passes on norms and values that benefit the ruling class and serve to maintain the **status quo**. They suggest that the family:

- reproduces labour power, that is, it produces future generations of workers
- is a unit of consumption (buying goods and services)
- offers emotional support for workers so that they can cope with the **exploitation** and frustrations of work
- socialises children so that inequality is seen as normal and inevitable.

So Marxists see the role of the family as helping to maintain an unfair and exploitative society without even realising it. Marxists say that because individuals internalise the norms and values of the ruling class, they are in a state of false consciousness, meaning that they are unaware that they are being exploited.

In short, Marxists see the family as beneficial to the ruling class but not to the subject class.

Grade boost

Find some examples and evidence to support the Marxist view of the family and some to criticise it. These are crucial in achieving a well-supported discussion and will boost your AO2 marks if used well.

quickfire

⑧ What criticisms can you make of the Marxist view of the family?

Key Terms

Patriarchal = male dominated.

Subordinate = in a less important position.

quickfire

⑨ Why do Feminists claim that families are bad for women? Is their view accurate?

Grade boost

Look for evidence that could be used to evaluate Feminist ideas about the family.

Key figure

Fran Ansley claims that the family transforms adult personalities into a patriarchal, capitalist framework. The emotional support provided by the wife acts as a safety valve for the frustration experienced by the husband in work.

Sociological debates and theories: Feminist ideas about the family

What do Feminists say about the family?

Feminists claim that society is **patriarchal**. A patriarchal society is one that is male dominated, one that is controlled by men for the benefit of men. Although there are several different branches of Feminism, most share the view that families are patriarchal institutions where women are oppressed by men. They also suggest that the family is an important source of gender role socialisation where females learn to be **subordinate** to men. Ann Oakley, writing in the 1970s, suggested that parents use a range of techniques to pass on messages about gender roles and these have important consequences for men and women during their lives. For example, it is claimed that gender socialisation in families teaches females to see child care and housework as female responsibilities.

Liberal feminists claim that marriage and family life is more beneficial to men than it is to women. Statistics show that married women have higher rates of morbidity than unmarried women. They are also likely to die at a younger age than unmarried women. Married men, on the other hand, live longer than unmarried men.

Madeleine Leonard (2000) found that boys and girls in her Belfast study did stereotypically male and female tasks when helping around the home. Boys, for example, were more likely to help with maintenance, whilst girls were more likely to help with domestic chores. Delphy and Leonard (1992) suggest that women are more likely than men to provide emotional support for the family and to sympathise with and flatter partners.

Male domination in families can also take the form of domestic violence with around 575,000 cases being reported each year plus an unknown number that go unreported. Women are often economically dependent on men. This dependency is partly the result of their domestic responsibilities, which mean that they are more likely to do part-time rather than full-time work.

In short, Feminists regard the family as an institution that is beneficial to men but not to women.

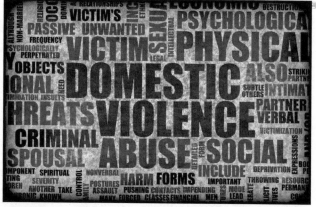

Feminists claim that traditional family life exploits and abuses women in a range of different ways.

The dark side of family life

Radical psychiatrists

Radical psychiatrists take a critical view of the family, claiming that it can be very damaging to individuals. Cooper, for example, suggests that families prevent people from thinking for themselves and as a result they are unable to realise their own potential. Laing is also very critical and he goes so far as to say that families are the source of many psychological problems such as schizophrenia and eating disorders.

Family life can be very unhappy for some children.

Violence in families

The existence of violence and abuse in families challenges the notion that the family is a safe haven for family members. Indeed, the family can, for some people, be a place of fear and insecurity. The reality of this **dark side of family life** has only come to light in relatively recent times. In the past such things might have been ignored because women and children had very little power, and it was more acceptable for a man to impose his authority. Violence is difficult to operationalise, for example smacking children was traditionally regarded as an acceptable aspect of parental discipline. However, as attitudes change it is more often regarded as an act of violence. Difficulties in operationalising the term violence make it difficult to measure. The British Crime Survey 2008 states that more than 1 in 20 of all crimes reported to the survey were classified as acts of **domestic violence**. Betsy Stanko estimates that an act of domestic violence is committed every six seconds. A 1998 BMA report stated that one in four women will experience domestic violence during their lives and this is more common during pregnancy. The NSPCC in 2000 stated that two children die every day at the hands of an abusive parent, and 6% of children suffer serious neglect. Men are also the victims of domestic abuse. A MORI poll in the mid 1990s revealed that 18% of men reported that they had been the victim of domestic violence and the real rate of domestic abuse against men is probably much higher.

Key Terms

Domestic violence = any form of violence that takes place in the home.

The dark side of family life = the damaging side of family life often hidden from view.

Grade boost

Understand the significance of the dark side of family life in discussions about the role of the family.

quickfire

(10) What does the dark side of family life suggest about the 'warm bath theory'?

Key figure

Sclater (2000) suggests that actual violence is easy to recognise but abuse and fear is also associated with the threat of violence. Behaviours such as verbal abuse, intimidation and psychological manipulation are not so easy to identify.

Key Terms

Conjugal relationships = the relationships between the two adult partners.

Segregated roles = roles are different.

Symmetrical relationships = those in which roles and responsibilities are shared equally between partners.

Grade boost

Use research evidence to argue for and against Willmott and Young's claim about symmetrical relationships.

The nature of conjugal roles and relationships can vary according to age and age of children.

quickfire

⑪ To what extent is there equality in conjugal relationships in contemporary society?

Key figure

Dryden (1999) claims that in a study of 17 married couples, women still had the main responsibility for housework and child care. Other studies confirm this to be the case even where the man is unemployed.

Relationships in families: conjugal relationships

Are conjugal relationships equal in contemporary society?

Willmott and Young in the 1970s claimed that **conjugal relationships** were becoming more **symmetrical** (equal), and this has been the source of much debate. Oakley was the first to dismiss this idea, stating that the findings of her own research showed a clear division of labour between men and women. Far from sharing domestic responsibilities and child care, as Willmott and Young suggest, Oakley found that women received little help and support from their husbands. Subsequent studies conducted since the 1970s have confirmed this **segregation** of conjugal roles. Indeed Allan and Crow (2001) suggest that even when women are engaged in paid employment their domestic responsibilities give them a dual burden. Edgell's research found similarly traditional patterns relating to decision making, with men more often making what were considered to be the more important decisions such as those relating to home finance. Similarly Vogel and Pahl's 1993 study suggested that some change in the control of finance had occurred but this change was directly linked to whether or not women were in paid employment.

Has structural diversity had an impact on relationships?

Even though more women are involved in paid employment, Duncombe and Marsden's 1990s research suggests that women are taking on a greater share of the burden than ever before. They call this the 'triple shift', in which women go out to work, look after the home and children and take on the responsibility for the emotional well-being of family members. There is some evidence of men becoming more involved in child care. Younger couples are more likely to share responsibilities and according to Weekes *et al.* there is evidence of equality in same sex relationships and Dunne confirms this in her study of cohabiting lesbian couples.

Violence, abuse and power

In relationships where violence is committed by one partner on the other there can be no equality. Indeed psychiatrists refer to 'learned helplessness' in which the abused partner has no self-esteem and as a result, loses the ability to change the situation.

In short, conjugal relationships continue on the whole to demonstrate inequality, though there is some evidence of change.

Relationships in families: parent–child relationships

Key Term

Economic liability = a drain on financial resources.

How are parent–child relationships changing?

Aries claimed that childhood is socially constructed and as such can change over time. In the latter part of the 19th century it was expected that a working-class child would leave school at 14, start work and begin to contribute to the family income. In this way children were an economic asset to the family. Children had few rights and they were 'seen and not heard'. Nowadays, children have their own rights, which have been written in law. The 1989 *Children's Act* stated that in the case of divorce the child's welfare must be of primary importance and the child must have a say in which parent they choose to live with. Children are now targeted by advertisers and, according to Buckingham, children influence adults through 'pester power'.

Single parenthood can have an effect on parent–child relationships.

Grade boost

Be aware that there are a number of factors that can have an impact on family forms and relationships, and these may not always be obvious.

quickfire

(12) In what ways can an increase in life expectancy have an impact on family structures and relationships?

Key figure

Scott (2004) argues that although children are said to be dependent for longer, they may be making important contributions to child care and housework. Children in lone parent families may be an important source of help and support to their parent. Children of immigrant parents may be translators for their parents.

Does childhood exist in 21st-century Britain?

Postman claims that childhood is only possible where the adult world and the child's world can be separated. The mass media makes this separation almost impossible and according to Postman this will inevitably result in the end of childhood. Buckingham disagrees and claims that children have become a significant economic force. Nick Lee (2001) suggests that childhood continues to exist but in a much more complex form. One in which, on the one hand, children are dependent on their parents (**economic liabilities**), and on the other, they have the power to make choices, particularly about what they buy.

How has the growing aged population affected relationships in families?

As the average life expectancy of both males and females increases, relationships change. For example, grandparent–grandchild relationships may become closer and grandparents may become more involved in the care of their grandchildren. On the other hand, as the health of elderly relatives deteriorates with age, a greater burden of care may be placed on their adult children. Family structures may change as elderly relatives may need to live with their adult children and such change inevitably has an impact of the dynamics of the family unit.

Families and Culture: Summary

Patterns and trends

Why has the rate of first-time marriages declined?

Marriage was for many years the basis of family life and the source of financial security for women. Sociologists are interested to understand why the popularity of first-time marriage seems to have declined and what the impact of this change might be.

Why has the divorce rate increased since the early 1970s?

The increase in divorce has led to new types of family, and Sociologists want to know why divorce has increased so that they can better understand social change.

What impact do changes in birth and death rates have on families and on society as a whole?

These demographic changes have had positive and negative effects on family life and on wider society. Sociology makes connections between these apparently disconnected social phenomena.

How does demographic change affect family life?

The changing role of women, changing attitudes about marriage and the growing ageing population can have an impact on roles and relationships in positive and negative ways.

Theories of family

Functionalists ...

...claim that most functional 'best fit' type of family is the traditional nuclear family that performs two irreducible functions.

The New Right ...

...take the same view but go further to suggest that families without fathers create poorly socialised children and delinquent boys.

Marxists ...

... believe that nuclear families are useful to a capitalist society. They pass on ruling class norms and values which help to keep workers in a state of false consciousness. They claim that nuclear families are good for capitalists but not for workers.

Feminists ...

... believe that families are patriarchal institutions that benefit men but exploit women and children.

Postmodernists ...

... suggest that the diversity of family types demonstrates that ways of thinking about family have changed and now people live in ways that they choose.

Debates

- What is the role of the family in society?
- Are families good for society and for individuals?
- Are relationships in families changing?
- Do families need fathers?
- Is the family in decline?

SY1 Youth Culture

The SY1 examination is concerned with how individuals become part of society and how social rules are made. The specification points out that youth cultures may be one route that people use to move from childhood to full adult status. We learn social rules, norms and values from others around us and young people may be more vulnerable to social pressure than adults who have gained a sense of their own place in society and have a sense of identity from working or being parents. Young people are often demonised by older people. You may expect questions to be directed at issues of identity, social change, social control and culture.

Revision checklist

Tick column 1 when you have completed brief revision notes.
Tick column 2 when you think you have a good grasp of the topic.
Tick column 3 during final revision when you feel you have mastery of the topic.

		1	2	3
p31 **What is youth culture?**	The origin of youth cultures			
	Characteristics of youth cultures			
p32 **What is the difference between youth culture and mainstream culture?**	Countercultures			
	Commitment			
p33 **The history of youth cultures**	Dates and styles			
	Identifying features			
	Main researchers and theorists			
p34 **Why do people join youth cultures?**	Rite of passage			
	Search for identity			
	Youth culture as a media creation			
	Resistance to authority			
p35 **Theories to explain youth culture**	Functionalism			
	Marxism			
	Interactionism			
	Postmodernism			
p36 **Youth culture and masculinity**	Traditional masculinity			
	New men and androgyny			
	Crisis of masculinity			
	Lads			

What is youth culture?

The origin of youth cultures

Youth cultures are a distinctive cultural phenomenon that developed after the end of the Second World War. For the first time, large numbers of young people had money to spend on themselves, and leisure time to enjoy themselves. In British cities in the 1950s, young men and some young women developed separate cultural identities away from their families and their local communities. They behaved in a way that was associated with neither childhood (toys and games) nor adulthood (family responsibilities). Older people were not accepted as part of these youth groups. Access to consumer goods such as fashions and American music became part of a new 'teen age' culture.

Characteristics of youth cultures

Many young people developed a distinctive way of dressing and behaving that led sociologists to describe them as youth culture. Some early youth cultures adopted dress codes and had accessories that made them stand out from other people, so they were described as 'spectacular youth cultures'. They were seen as shocking to people who did not follow the **styles** and were often presented by media as being threatening to society because they appeared to reject traditional norms and values.

Characteristics of youth cultures included distinctive taste in fashions, hairstyles, music, slang words, dance styles, use of leisure drugs and vehicles (motorbikes, motor scooters or cars and vans). Some youth cultures attracted large numbers of young people who followed the fashions, whereas others were only open to small numbers of people, for reasons of social class, gender or ethnicity.

What image of himself is this young man attempting to pass on to other people?

Grade boost

It is helpful to remember that some sociologists see youth cultures as being separate and distinctive from ordinary culture, whereas others see youth cultures as a phase that some, though not all young people pass through.

quickfire

① Why did the first youth cultures develop?

Key figure

Phil Cohen (1972) argued that for some youth cultures, their cultural tastes had significance and social meaning (substance) whereas other youth cultures were simply interested in style and looks.

Key Terms

Mainstream culture = the culture that is traditional and which most people follow.

Counterculture = a youth culture that rejects or opposes traditional values.

Grade boost

Note that if most young people are absorbed into a particular fashion or style, for example by clubbing or drug taking, then to what extent is the culture they belong to actually different from mainstream culture?

quickfire

② In what ways are youth cultures separate and different from mainstream society?

Key figures

Sociologists at the Centre for Contemporary Cultural Studies (CCCS) (1964–2002) in Birmingham claimed that young working-class people joined youth cultures because they rejected the middle-class cultural values of mainstream society.

What is the difference between youth culture and mainstream culture?

Mainstream culture is the term that refers to the traditional values of a society. Most people in a society would form mainstream culture. Youth cultures tend only to be open to young people. There is a debate in Sociology as to whether youth cultures are just a normal part of growing up in our society (Parsons) or they are something different and special to young people.

Some youth cultures have differing values from mainstream culture, embracing drug use or crime as part of the expected lifestyle, although they share values with most people. American 'gangsta' culture, for example, values wealth and status as do many Americans, but participants are expected to achieve these things through criminal activity.

Countercultures

Some youth cultures are antagonistic or rejecting of traditional or mainstream cultures. These cultures are described as **counterculture**s. Countercultures may challenge authority through protest or through adopting values that reject mainstream culture. Hippies in the 1960s and 1970s talked of 'dropping out' of society and many went on to explore 'alternative' lifestyles. They protested against the Vietnam War and created festivals and magazines to promote their viewpoints.

Most countercultures are short lived. The ideas and fashions become adopted by mainstream culture and commercialised. Eventually, they are seen as normal or just a style people can buy into. In the 1990s, Wyn and White (1997) suggested that most young people are not deeply committed to a particular subculture, even though they like the style.

This logo from 1960s summarises the values of the hippy culture.

Commitment

Some young people are more deeply committed to the ideals and values of youth cultures than others. So, for some young people, the youth culture becomes part of their identity, whereas for others, it is no more than a way of being social. Bennett has identified that many people retain a commitment for the music and styles of their youth well beyond their thirties.

The history of youth cultures

Date	Classification of styles	Identifying features	Studied by
1950s–60s	Teddy Boys	Alcohol, Edwardian clothes, rock and roll	Hall and Jefferson Hopkins
	Beat generation	Cigarettes, alcohol, marijuana	
	Rockers	Motorbikes, leather, alcohol, rock'n'roll	Stanley Cohen
	Mods	Amphetamines, scooters, mohair suits and parkas, soul music	Stanley Cohen Dick Hebdige
1960–70s	Hippies	Progressive rock, cannabis and LSD, peasant styles and Asian style, long hair	Paul Willis
	Skinheads	Short tight jeans, shaved heads, racism, Doc Martens boots, ska music	John Clarke
	Rasta (Black youth culture)	Cannabis, reggae, dreadlocks, religious affiliation to Jamaica, respect for body (foods)	
1980s	New Romantic/ New Wave	Amphetamines, androgyny, historical fantasy dress and cosmetics, Glam rock	
	Punk	Anarchists, spiky hair, ripped clothes, glue-sniff, piercings, punk music, bondage clothes	Dick Hebdige Iain Chambers Michael Maffesoli
1990s	Hip-hop	Baggy pants, designer clothes, rap, trainers, cannabis, cocaine, Black culture	
	Grunge	Heavy rock, ripped and dirty clothing, heroin	
	Rave (Dance culture)	Clubbing, ecstasy and designer drugs, cocaine, garage, Bhangra, remix, comfortable shoes, light sticks, baggy pants, loud colour	Sarah Thornton
	Goths	Piercings, black, death metal, androgyny	Paul Hodkinson
2000 –	Chavs/townies	Cannabis, alcohol, sports clothes, Hip hop, R'n'B, heavy jewellery	
	Emo	Cannabis, sexual blurring, emotional rock, dyed black hair, thick glasses, anorexic thinness	Paul Hodkinson

Key Terms

Urban Tribes = term used by Maffesoli (1985) to describe small groups of people in cities who develop a particular style and way of living. Many youth cultures develop from these small and style conscious groups.

Grade boost

Note that classifying youth cultures can be complex because many styles evolve out of the fashions of previous generations; Skinhead probably developed from Mod styles and Emo developed from Goth styles.

quickfire

③ What recent youth cultures can you describe? What are the styles they use to identify themselves?

Key figure

Mike Brake (1980) claims that youth cultures are individual responses to major social problems; people join a group to give themselves a sense of identity.

Key Terms

Consumerism = an attitude that people should spend money and purchase goods, perhaps to excess.

Capitalistic = describes a social system based around wealth and profit from selling goods.

Grade boost

There is a variety of views for you to consider in this topic and you may need to evaluate the usefulness of each, with appropriate evidence from research.

quickfire

④ Why do young people join youth cultures?

Key figure

Paul Willis (1998) claims that young people are often interested in style and fashion because they are not able to access traditional art. They are forced to express their creativity in new and different ways which he terms, symbolic creativity.

Why do people join youth cultures?

Rite of passage

Many sociologists, particularly Functionalists, argue that there is no clear boundary between childhood and adulthood, so young people involve themselves in youth cultures. An extreme position suggests that people are attracted to youth cultures because their families failed to socialise them correctly as children, so they are not ready to become full adults.

A Bar Mizvah is a rite of passage where a young Jewish male celebrates the end of his childhood and his new status as a man.

Search for identity

Another popularly held view is that youth cultures are attractive because people develop a sense of personal identity through adopting the styles and values of youth cultures. As jobs are scarce and education difficult, young people choose alternative ways of gaining status and a sense of belonging to society. Youth cultures can provide this. Mac n Ghaill (1994), for example, claims that young men are attracted to youth cultures to emphasise their masculinity.

Youth culture as a media creation

Stan Cohen (1972) claims that the media romanticise and exaggerate youth cultures, so young people are attracted to the lifestyle and attitudes portrayed. They imitate and associate themselves with the ideas. Some youth cultures are **consumerist** because they encourage people to buy items associated with the style. However, Roberts (1997) says that while companies sell 'youthfulness' as an idea associated with products, they are increasingly careful not to target any age group, so computer games are sold to adults as well as teenage boys.

Resistance to authority

Marxists suggest that youth cultures are a form of rebellion. Stuart Hall and Tony Jefferson (1979) argue that young people are attracted to youth cultures as a way of rejecting **capitalistic** society. This, they suggest, explains why some youth cultures appear threatening to authority and why some young people act in a manner that is deliberately shocking.

Theories to explain youth culture

As Sociology has developed there have been a variety of theories that have developed to explain youth culture. Within each tradition in Sociology there have been debates and discussions so that a number of viewpoints have been put forward.

Functionalism

American sociologists in the Functionalist tradition were among the first sociologists to look at youth cultures. They viewed adolescence as a period of transition between childhood and adulthood. Some writers in this tradition saw young people as a problem because they had different values from their parents and took on **deviant** behaviours. Others see youth cultures as simply a phase that young people pass through.

Marxism

Marxists are very concerned with class divisions in society and how society is controlled by the wealthy and powerful for their own interests. They tend to see youth cultures as a form of **resistance** to the cultural ideas of the **elite**. They claimed that subcultures tend to form in inner city areas where there is high unemployment and social unrest. Brake and others believe that youth subcultures provide '**magical**' solutions because membership gives people the freedom to experiment with ideas.

Interactionism

Interactionists do not look at the whole of society, but they do focus on relationships. Much of their work has been done by people investigating youth gangs and deviant groups. It is claimed that young people join gangs and groups as a source of identity. Becker suggests that young people are targeted by the police and authority figures so they develop a deviant identity for themselves, defining themselves as different from mainstream society.

Postmodernism

This is an influential recent approach to Sociology. It suggests that people now mix styles, music and ideas. They can choose what to believe and what to reject. Instead of belonging to a wide subculture such as the Hippies appeared to be, young people develop neotribes or urban tribes. Here, the style is more important than the values. They may even adopt the styles of previous youth cultures without a sense of their meaning.

Key Terms

Elite = powerful people in society.

Deviant = someone who breaks social rules.

Resistance = a Marxist idea, it describes the way that people reject traditional social values of the middle classes and invent their own cultural ideas.

Magic theory = youth cultures provide a form of solution to the problems of society for their members.

Grade boost

Social theory is very important to Sociology and it will be helpful if you can recognise the theories and the type of language used by the writers from each perspective.

quickfire

(5) Provide a list of strengths and weaknesses of each viewpoint. These should be supported with evidence, where relevant.

Key figure

Zygmunt Bauman (1992), a postmodernist, claims that young people are caught between the desire of commercial companies to make them consumers of goods such as alcohol, and traditional culture which criticises them and acts to prevent them doing what they wish.

Youth culture and masculinity

Key Terms

Lad = a form of sport mad, joking, cool masculinity.

Crisis of masculinity = boys no longer know what behaviour is expected of them as men.

Exaggerated masculinity = excessively aggressive and sexualised male behaviour.

Grade boost

You may need to assess just how much masculine behaviour has changed, or even if it has changed since the first youth cultures developed in the 1950s.

quickfire

⑥ Why have some youth cultures challenged traditional gender patterns, whereas others reinforced them?

Key figure

Germaine Greer is an influential feminist. She, like many other radical feminists, sees aggressively masculine behaviour as being a problem for society as it leads to major social problems and lawlessness.

This image shows characteristics that are more commonly seen as masculine in our society.

Traditional masculinity

Some writers have suggested that youth cultures are masculine in nature because males are dominant. It is possible that girls were overlooked by early researchers. However, many early youth cultures were associated with males and some showed signs of **exaggerated masculinity** through expressions of violence and disregard of women. Osgerby (1997) says that before the 1950s males were expected to look after women; however, youth cultures and media stereotypes encouraged men to take on a more sexist and aggressive role.

New men and androgyny

Androgyny refers to the blurring of sexual boundaries. In the 1960s and 1970s, both men and women challenged traditional gender roles in society. The media identified the New Man who was in touch with his feminine side. Some youth cultures of the 1970s challenged traditional male roles, so male Hippies wore their hair long. Working-class youth cultures are more likely to be masculine, whereas middle-class youth cultures tend to be androgynous.

This young man is androgynous because he has adopted styles that are typical of young females.

Crisis of masculinity

It has been argued by Connell (1995) and others that men found their traditional roles challenged and young men in particular felt threatened by the rise of females. This led to boys developing a number of different forms of masculinity. Sewell (1997) claimed that Black boys in London responded to racism through emphasising a culture of cool sexuality.

Lads

A new form of masculinity has been identified. **Lads** are boys who are interested in maintaining cool through interest and ability in sport and messing around. Greer claims that this culture has emerged as a reaction against the changing social position of women in our culture.

Others have argued that the New Man never really existed and that the hard drinking, sporty, car mad lad is actually a continuation of a male tradition that never really went away. Boys find this form of masculine expression more attractive than the New Man ideal.

Youth culture and girls

Girls are relatively understudied in youth culture. Most ethnographies focus on males, so the extent of female involvement in youth culture is little understood. Male youth culture takes place on the streets; girls are thought to be more confined to the home.

Bedroom culture

McRobbie and Garber (1975) identified a '**bedroom culture**'. Girls spent time in each other's houses, engaging in feminine activities such as reading magazines and chatting. This was to do with dual sexual morality; girls attract criticism and gain a bad reputation if they participated in activities that were normal for men. This work was published over thirty years ago and norms for male and female behaviours have changed.

More recently, Hey (1997) conducted a study of girls' friendships through the notes they sent each other in class. She found that girls learn to survive being subordinate in society through their friendships with each other.

Ladettes

A new feminine identity known as the **ladette** has emerged. Ladettes are girls who act like males. Ladettes are seen as promiscuous and a problem for society. Jackson (2006) found that ladette and lad culture develops in schools through a fear of academic failure.

Girl gangs

The phenomenon of the girl gang is mostly American, where gang culture is more common than in the UK. Archer (1998) has claimed that the numbers of girls involved in such gang-related criminal activities are growing, but points out that there has not been enough research into the topic. Girl gangs organise themselves along the same lines as male gangs: they have leaders, are associated with a geographical location, spend time together and engage in illegal activity. They may wear an identifiable style of clothing and hair. Wilson said that girls in gangs were resisting traditional female roles.

'New' bedroom culture

Although sociologists still talk about bedroom culture, this term is now related to the use of the Internet in individual bedrooms where young people create websites and use social networking and chat sites to create new 'virtual' youth cultures. Again, girls are heavily identified as being part of the new web-communities.

To what extent are modern teenage girls part of a bedroom culture of make-up and chats about romance and relationships?

Key Terms

Bedroom culture = girls meet in their rooms to chat and form friendships.

'New' bedroom culture = people sit in private but create online communities and friendships.

Ladettes = girls who behave like boys.

Grade boost

Is it true that girls are becoming more laddish, or even if this is a completely new behaviour? It may simply be an aspect of women's behaviour that was previously overlooked or suppressed by men.

quickfire

⑦ How do male and female subcultures differ? In what ways are they the same?

Key figure

Frith (1983) identified the Teenybopper culture of young girls and suggested that it was commercial in origin and more focused on pop stars than pop music. This is a preparation for the later romantic attachment to boyfriends.

Youth culture and social class

Key Terms

Disaffected = people who feel dissatisfied and not fully part of society.

Consumer goods = items people wish to buy, such as clothing, music and media products.

Grade boost

Whilst young people probably identify with certain fashions and groups, it is probably fair to say that no single youth culture exists. Some youth styles are more attractive to working-class youth than middle-class youth. Middle classes copy street style, whereas working classes aspire to middle-class consumer goods.

quickfire

⑧ Is social class an important element in youth culture?

Can you identify the social class of these young people? What clues would you use to guess?

Key figure

Willis (1978) claims that spectacular youth cultures will not reappear. Biker gangs in the 1970s had more sense of loyalty than modern young people do to their styles. Today's youth subcultures point to a pick'n'mix of style in terms of gender, class and age.

Working-class youth cultures

Many of the early spectacular youth cultures (Teds, Mods and Rockers) originated in working-class urban areas. Abrams, writing in the 1950s claimed that they developed because the working classes had disposable income and could spend it on leisure goods. These cultures were seen as threatening by the media. Their adoption of unusual clothing, use of alcohol and drugs and some violent behaviours, led to moral panics. Eisenstadt, a Functionalist, saw youth cultures as a problem caused by poor socialisation in working-class families.

In the 1970s, Phil Cohen and the CCCS argued that working-class young people developed youth cultures as a way of 'magically' recreating the values and experiences of older generations, thus Skinhead fashion was an exaggeration of working-class styles. Hebdige saw punk as a conscious rejection of **consumerism**, but nevertheless, shops sold punk style. Hebdige saw this as a way that capitalism has of defusing the rebellion of youth culture, making it safe to consume by those who are not part of it, but hangers on.

The recent moral panics surrounding Chavs and Hoodies could be seen as fear of the potential for danger from **disaffected** working-class youth. Both words are terms of abuse and not used by people who subscribe to the fashions.

Middle-class youth cultures

Hippie culture developed in the USA among university students who objected to the Vietnam War and rejected consumer society. Marxist writers in the 1970s tended to dismiss the influence of the Hippie culture as being middle class and were less interested in studying it. Nevertheless, it was a powerful influence on many young people.

Changes to class and culture

Roberts and Parsell (1990s) found little evidence of class awareness among young people and little link between class and youth cultures. Middle-class youth had more leisure time to devote to social activity and more money to spend on **consumer goods**. The middle classes therefore dominate fashion and style. Postmodernism suggests that class allegiance has broken down and that people now belong to urban tribes.

Youth culture and ethnicity

The sociology of youth culture tends to be **ethnocentric**, meaning the focus is on white youth groups rather than other cultural groups. However, the relationship between youth cultures and minority ethnic groups is a complex one. Youth cultures have an uneasy relationship with ethnic minorities. They tend to draw on Black music and other ethnic styles, whilst some youth cultures have also been very racist in behaviour; Skinheads listened to Jamaican music but were famed for overt racism and 'Paki-bashing'.

Globalisation

Globalisation is the process of different cultures and economies becoming more aware of each other to combine into a worldwide culture. Young people are more aware of other cultures and especially American culture. In the 1950s, Teddy boys listened to American Rock music, much of it performed by Blacks. British young people are influenced by modern American music such as rap and hip-hop. Eastern religions were an influence on the values and beliefs of the Hippies.

Ethnic subcultures

There have been a number of youth cultures that have originated among ethnic minority communities. Partly, ethnic minorities form their own groups because they are excluded from the fashions and styles of whites. Asian young people created Bhangra; a fusion of Punjabi, reggae and rap music. This mix of an ethnic and a mainstream culture is known as a **hybrid culture**.

White commercialisation of Black street style

The relationship between ethnic minorities and youth culture is further complicated because Black and other styles and music have been taken over by white people and commercialised. Rastafarianism originated in Jamaica as a response to white repression, but the music (reggae) is now widely enjoyed. Furthermore, the bands that made reggae music popular were often white. The Rasta hairstyle of Dreadlocks is now a fashion choice rather than a political statement for many people.

Young black styles and moves are often adopted by middle-class white youth who are looking for a bit of 'edge' or a dangerous image.

Key Terms

Hybrid culture = a fusion between two cultures to create a new cultural form.

Globalisation = the process of cultures becoming more aware of each other.

Ethnocentric = putting one's own culture first.

Grade boost

Many youth groups draw on ideas from other cultures; Black Americans have been especially influential over a number of years, especially their music. Nevertheless, the influence of ethnic minority groups is not always recognised, even by the people who enjoy their contribution to popular culture.

quickfire

⑨ To what extent are members of ethnic minority groups accepted by mainstream white youth cultures?

Key figure

Dick Hebdige (1976) identified Skinheads as being a traditional white, working-class, male movement which felt threatened by mass immigration at a time of great social unrest. This resulted in aggressive racism and identification with Right Wing movements such as the BNP.

The changing nature of youth culture

Key Terms

Spectacular youth culture = a distinctive youth subculture with a specific style and set of values.

Neotribe = a loose gathering of people with similar tastes and interests.

Consumerism = an attitude based on gaining status and pleasure from buying and using goods.

Grade boost

Questions on changing youth culture require more than a description of changes in style and taste. Changes to youth culture reflect changes to the whole of society and your writing should display understanding of this point.

quickfire

⑩ What are the differences between a spectacular youth culture and a neotribe?

Key figure

Giddens is one of the best known sociologists and theorists in the UK. He has been influential in politics and advised the Labour government 1997 – 2010. He asks an interesting question; how is it that early youth cultures were so critical of society and yet have had such limited influence on wider social change?

Spectacular youth culture

Early youth cultures appeared to arise spontaneously in working-class areas of cities, mostly London. They had distinctive dress and styles that were outrageous and somewhat threatening to older people. Thus, early youth cultures were described as spectacular. There were even periods when no youth culture was dominant, so in the late 1950s, Teddy Boy culture was declining whilst Mod or Rocker culture had not yet developed. Clarke and Jefferson pointed out that these youth cultures were more than just a fashion statement for the participants – to be a Mod meant subscribing to a specific world view.

Commercialisation

By the late 1960s and 1970s, some youth cultures and relatively short-lived fads such as 'Glam rock' were initiated by commercial companies selling media products and fashions to young people. In addition, there was an increasing degree of classlessness about some of these youth cultures, so that although Hippies tended to be middle class, working-class youth would adopt the styles. By the 2000s, Archer found that working-class youth were spending upwards of £40 a week to buy style goods and were sometimes attracted to crime to buy high status brands.

Gender changes

In the 1950s, gender differences were clearly understood by both sexes. There were traditional patterns of male dominance and female domestication. Changing norms and values have left young men and women unsure of their place in society. Giddens (2009) and Bauman (1997, 1993) both suggest that girls and boys are under pressure to create personal identities. Girls are now excelling in traditional male areas and some are becoming ladettes; some boys react by becoming aggressively masculine. Others are openly accepting gay identities.

Neotribes and postmodernism

Modern youth cultures are often based on **consumerism**. People can buy into styles and clothing. Whereas early youth cultures were subcultures with clear social rules, modern youth cultures are not so structured. Bennett (2006) has talked about young people as forming tribes, describing them as a loose-knit coming-together of people with similar interests, so there are events such as 'Tribal Gathering'. Rave, for example, allows a wider age range and ethnic minorities to participate.

The representation of youth in the media

The media creates our 'other'

The media have become the major socialising force in our culture (Kellner 1995). They help us create cultural identities, providing us with a sense of what we are, and a sense of what we are not (**other**). This means that we separate ourselves from other people because we are not like them – we feel we are somehow different or better.

Angels and demons

Early social commentators on youth viewed young people as a problem for society. Their behaviour was exaggerated and seen as dangerous. They were subjected to social control through the courts. It is argued that youth groups have taken on the status of other; they are demonised by newspapers and become **folk devils**. The public reaction is known as a **moral panic**.

Folk devils and moral panics

In the 1970s Stan Cohen conducted a study of the relationship between the media and the youth groups known as Mods and Rockers. He described a process whereby a small incident on a news-free weekend was over-reported and this created a public backlash against the Mods and Rockers. Courts and the police were overly harsh in dealing with the 'problem'. In reporting the story, the newspapers also described the styles of the youth groups, so other young people were attracted to the behaviour and began to participate themselves.

Modern representations

McRobbie and Thornton (1995) pointed out that members of the rave scene known as Acid House enjoyed being misrepresented by the media because this reinforced their view of themselves as being somehow exciting and more dangerous than they really were.

Youth culture as a media creation

Young people are a market for consumer goods such as fashion, media products and music. Schor (1992) says that the increased leisure spending of households has meant that young people are encouraged to lead the 'cool' lifestyles portrayed by the media and do not develop critical skills to challenge some negative ideas that are put forward. They buy into a media-created youth culture that depends on exploitation of poor countries without recognising the implications of their purchasing power.

Key Terms

Other = we define ourselves as being 'not like' people we disapprove of, who are the other.

Folk devils = a group in society that people disapprove of.

Moral panic = the process by which the media whip up the authorities into over-reacting against a social phenomenon.

Grade boost

What examples of modern moral panics attached to young people can you identify?

quickfire

⑪ What is the process by which a youth group becomes a folk devil?

Key figure

Osgerby (2004) points out that there can be a racist element to the creation of folk devils. In the early 2000s, a moral panic developed about young black men and gun crime, with the targets of the media being the negative influence of rap music and violent computer games.

This girl would have seemed dangerous and shocking in the 1960s when these styles became popular with Mods.

Key Terms

Counterculture = an anti-authority subculture that may involve itself in criminal behaviours.

ASBO = antisocial behaviour order, a legal control mechanism to prevent antisocial behaviour.

Social inclusion = degree of participation in society.

Grade boost

Sociological and media concern with viewing young people as a problem or looking at spectacular behaviours means that the vast majority of mainstream young people tend to get overlooked and ignored in debates and discussions.

quickfire

⑫ How have the lives of young people and adolescents changed over the past fifty years?

Key figure

Gill Jones has been conducting a major study into youth and pathways into adulthood for the Joseph Rowntree Foundation since 1997. Over 20 individual projects have been carried out. She has discovered major social inequalities along social class lines which affect life chances for young people.

The changing status of young people in society

Whilst youthfulness is admired in our culture, young people are often not treated with respect or valued. There are various issues that are particularly relevant to young people.

Joblessness

The job situation for young people has been difficult since the 1980s and before. Recent statistics show that the unemployment rates among young people are higher than for other age groups in the UK. The youth unemployment rate is 17%, more than twice the national average. Those without qualifications are most likely to experience difficulties getting work, but even those with qualifications are likely to be underemployed or unemployed.

Social inclusion

Park *et al.* (1995) found that political involvement has declined since the 1990s. Support for and knowledge of politics has also declined, even though large numbers of young people felt they should be consulted about political decisions that affect their lives. Few had been involved in charity work or political protest, though most had been out, mostly to the cinema.

Attitudes to family

Again, Park and others have found that young people today have liberal attitudes to sexuality and sexual behaviours, though boys are more traditional in their viewpoints than girls. Many have been brought up with the experience of broken families and Murray says they do not have appropriate role models for life.

Social control

Cieslik suggested in 2007 that increasing moral panics over young people's behaviour have led to government policy initiatives that have increased the degree of control in society: **ASBO**s, curfews, school discipline and community policing are all targeted at the young. On one hand they are given freedoms, but on the other they are treated severely if they infringe rules.

The value of education

Husen (1979) and others such as Jackson point out that the increasingly high value placed on educational qualifications in our society has led to a split in the cultures of young people. Those with low educational qualifications are likely to remain unemployed and unemployable. They are more likely to develop criminal **counterculture**s

Deviance and youth culture

Deviant behaviours and countercultures

Most youth cultures are deviant in the sense that they adopt dress codes and behaviours that go against the norms of society. Some countercultures have been associated with deviant behaviours that are criminal: most youth cultures have had favoured leisure drugs. Many have used alcohol but some used illegal drugs. Mods were associated with amphetamines, Hippies with cannabis and rave culture with ecstasy and cocaine among other drugs. A number of studies (Sanders 2006) have reported increasing non-medical use of a variety of drugs to the point where it may also be a norm among youth groups, particularly those attending clubs and raves. Authorities are concerned about the health **risks** and a number of strategies have been put in place to inform young people as well as to reduce usage.

Youth cultures and delinquency

Youth itself is seen as a problem by many researchers into crime. Young people have high conviction rates for crime and criminal behaviours. Youth crime is known as delinquency and there have been many studies of **delinquent** groups including James Patrick's famous study of a Glasgow street gang. Delinquency has often been associated with areas of cities that are deprived; where poverty and lack of work means that young people do not feel part of society. Rutter, in 1995, claimed that the rise in global delinquency came about because of separate youth cultures. May suggested that young people mature earlier but that adult responsibility is delayed. They form delinquent cultures as part of a transition period. They lack control but desire consumer goods.

Anti-school subcultures

Many delinquent groups and subcultures originate in schools, and educationalists have been concerned with the process that creates anti-school subcultures. In the 1950s, Downes said that school is meaningless for many working-class youths and they protect themselves by rejecting an education system that has rejected them. In the 1960s, Hargreaves wrote about children being labelled as failures by schools and forming delinquent subcultures. The CCCS described anti-school cultures as being a rejection of the dominant middle-class values of school. Mac an Ghaill described 'macho lads' who look and act smart and value their mates.

Key Terms

Risk behaviour = this is behaviour that is dangerous such as binge drinking or drug abuse.

Delinquent = young criminal.

Grade boost

Youthful deviance is seen as a problem by the media and some functionalists, a natural process of growing up by other functionalists. Marxists see it as resistance to capitalism and postmodernists see it as a lifestyle choice.

quickfire

⑬ To what extent are youth subcultures deviant?

Key figure

Albert Cohen (1950s) said that those most likely to commit deviant acts were found in the lower streams of schools and living in deprived areas. Such boys were aware of being branded failures by the school. Groups of such boys formed because they were denied regular routes to status.

Cannabis was the illegal drug of choice for Hippies.

Youth Culture: Summary

We have identified the key points of this topic on the WJEC AS specification, i.e. the bare minimum you need to know. You may want to fill in further details to elaborate and personalise this content.

Theories to explain youth culture

Functionalists...

...say that it is just a transitional stage that people pass through between childhood and full adult status.

Marxists...

...say that youth cultures are a form of working-class resistance to capitalism.

Interactionists...

...say that young people wear distinctive clothing and fashion; this leads to negative labelling as deviant. The young people then become reinforced in their attitudes and behaviour.

Feminists...

...say that girls are overlooked by malestream sociologists, but they have youth cultures of their own.

Postmodernists...

...say that the spectacular youth cultures of the pre-1980s have given way to neotribes where style is more important than subcultural norms and values.

The nature of youth culture

How did they begin?

There is some debate as to whether youth cultures existed before the 1950s, but the first well-documented youth cultures started after the Second World War.

What are youth subcultures?

These are groups with distinct lifestyles, behaviour and interests. Older people are not expected to participate.

What are the characteristics of youth cultures?

Members of youth cultures share a sense of style, a taste in music and leisure drugs and have values that appear to threaten mainstream culture.

What are spectacular youth cultures?

These are youth cultures that act in a dramatic way with styles that are intended to shock and annoy. Examples were Hippies and Punks.

What is counterculture?

Some youth cultures are challenging and threatening to dominant values.

What is a neotribe?

This is a contemporary phenomenon where styles and fashions are said to be fluid and people's sense of belonging to the youth group tends to be short lived.

Are youth cultures significant?

Yes, they may be

- There is a lot of public concern about some youth cultures and the behaviour of youth.
- The mass media often sell newspapers offering a very negative view of young people suggesting that their behaviour is deviant.
- Many youth cultures attract racist, sexist or violent elements.

No, they aren't

- Not all young people join youth cultures or even take them seriously.
- Some youth cultures have been positive in changing people's attitudes, for example ecowarriors have raised consciousness about the environment.
- Many youth cultures are harmless and people grow away from them as they settle down.

SY2 Research Methods

When revising research methods, you should focus on the main debates and issues surrounding the use of methods. For example, you should have a basic understanding of the broad theoretical approaches of positivism, interpretivism and realism that underpin sociological research. In exam questions examiners may ask questions about the strengths and weaknesses of different methods such as questionnaires, interviews, observation and using secondary data. In addition, you need to grasp the qualities of, as well as the motives for collecting qualitative and quantitative data. You should be able to link this to how specific research methods are appropriate to the collection of qualitative or quantitative data. You should also be aware of issues such as reliability, validity, generalisability and representativeness and how these apply to the research process. Finally, you should be aware of the ethical and practical problems associated with undertaking sociological research.

Revision checklist

Tick column 1 when you have completed brief revision notes.
Tick column 2 when you think you have a good grasp of the topic.
Tick column 3 during final revision when you feel you have mastery of the topic.

		1	2	3
p47 **What is the sociological approach to research?**	Quantitative approach			
	Qualitative approach			
	Primary data			
	Secondary data			
p48 **What are the key ideas of sociological research?**	Reliability			
	Validity			
	Representativeness and generalisability			
p49 **What are the ethical issues of research?**	Informed consent			
	Preserve confidentiality			
	Effects on people being studied			
	Competence			
p50 **What practical problems are associated with research?**	Financial			
	Time			
	Researchers' careers			
	Choice of methods			
	Proximity to respondents			

			1	2	3
p51	**What is meant by sampling?**	Random sampling			
		Stratified random sampling			
		Quota sampling			
		Systematic sampling			
		Snowball sampling			
p52	**Why do Sociologists use questionnaires?**	Characteristics of questionnaires			
		Advantages of questionnaires			
		Disadvantages of questionnaires			
p53	**Why do Sociologists use interviews?**	Characteristics of interviews			
		Structured interviews			
		Unstructured interviews			
		Advantages of interviews			
		Disadvantages of interviews			
p54	**Why do Sociologists use observation?**	Overt observation			
		Covert observation			
		Advantages of observation			
		Disadvantages of observation			
p55	**Why do Sociologists use other secondary sources?**	Previous sociological research			
		Documents			
		Media sources			
		Advantages of secondary sources			
		Disadvantages of secondary sources			
p56	**Why do Sociologists use official statistics?**	Benefits of official statistics			
		Problems with official statistics			
		Sociological perspectives and official statistics			

What is the sociological approach to research?

The subject matter of Sociology is about the relationships people make with each other. These take place within the context of the social institutions (family, education, etc.) that make up the culture or society in which they live. Sociological research is important as it gives us more than a common-sense understanding of the social world in which we live. By undertaking rigorous and evidence-based research most sociologists claim their findings are objective and value free. This is particularly true of the **quantitative** approach.

Quantitative approach

The early classical sociologists of 19th century modelled their research on the methods of the natural sciences. This approach, known as positivism, argued that sociologists should only study observable phenomena. Emile Durkheim (1865–1917) pioneered this approach with his statistical study of suicide. The quantitative approach involves collecting numerical data and social facts, establishing **correlations** (links between social phenomena) and searching for '**cause and effect**' relationships.

Qualitative approach

Whereas the quantitative approach sees reality as objective and measurable through statistics, the **qualitative** approach is favoured by interpretive sociologists who see reality as more subjective. The classical sociologist Max Weber (1864–1920) argued that in order to give meaning to people's actions we should practise '*verstehen*' which literally means 'understand' but in practice involves empathising by putting yourself in the shoes of those you are researching. Thus, the qualitative approach is very much a people-centred approach to research collecting word-centred data.

Primary data

Primary data is collected directly by the sociologists as part of their research. The methods used for this include surveys (using questionnaires or interviews), observation and occasionally experiments.

Secondary data

Secondary data is used by sociologists but collected by organisations or other people. Examples of secondary data include official statistics, previous research, historical and personal documents and diaries.

Key Terms

Cause and effect = when one thing directly leads to the other.

Correlation = when a statistical relationship exists between two things.

Quantitative methods = methods used by Positivists, such as social surveys, to obtain empirical data usually in the form of statistics.

Qualitative methods = non-positivistic approach to obtain in-depth understanding of human behaviour and the reasons behind that behaviour.

Grade boost

An awareness of the realist approach, which recognises that the strengths of one approach cancel out the weaknesses of the other, is useful when discussing the relative merits of the quantitative and qualitative approaches. This ties in with the practice of methodological pluralism.

quickfire

① Why is it important to move beyond a common-sense understanding of the social world?

Key figure

Emile Durkheim (1897) undertook a quantitative study of official statistics on suicide across Europe in an attempt to scientifically identify the social facts that caused high or low suicide rates in different countries.

Key Terms

Reliable = when research is replicable and would get the same results.

Valid = true to life.

Representative = when a sample has the same characteristics as the target population.

Generalisability = when findings from a sample can be said to reflect the social characteristics of target population or wider society.

Grade boost

Always avoid writing in an exam answer that research was 'both reliable and valid' in the same sentence. As noted above there tends to be a trade-off between the two, with one being higher when it is lower in the other.

quickfire

② Why is it important for sociological research to be reliable?

Key figure

Max Weber: challenged the scientific approach of positivism, arguing that studying human beings was not the same as objects. Instead he encouraged an interpretive approach centred on understanding the meanings behind people's actions.

What are the key ideas of sociological research?

Given that sociology is trying to explain human behaviour, it is essential that all sociological research is of the highest quality. Sound conclusions can only be drawn from good quality evidence. However, the sociologist's subject matter (people) is unpredictable as people do not necessarily always tell the truth. This is sometimes accidental but can also be down to a desire on their part to present themselves in the best possible light. Sociologists use the measures of **reliability** and **validity** in order to evaluate the quality of evidence from their own or other research.

Reliability

Reliability is often a difficult concept to grasp, but is actually quite a simple idea; meaning that if the researcher (or anyone else) was to repeat the research then the same results would be obtained. The quantitative approach is generally viewed as being high in reliability but lower in validity. In terms of research methods, carefully constructed questionnaires tend to produce data that is higher in reliability than other methods.

Validity

Validity is an essential characteristic of good research; meaning that it is true to life. Validity generally derives from respondents being honest about their behaviour and feelings. However, it can also be influenced by the poor design of the research procedure. In addition, the researcher can affect validity through being biased or from drawing unjustified conclusions from the data collected. Qualitative research is generally viewed as being higher in validity and lower in reliability, although it is clearly important that both quantitative and qualitative research is accurate and true to life. In terms of research methods, unstructured interviews and observations tend to produce data that is higher in validity than other methods.

Representativeness and generalisability

Representativeness refers to the characteristics of any sample that is used in relation to the target population being studied. If they do not share the same characteristics and in the same proportions then it is not possible to draw any meaningful generalisations from the research. **Generalisability** is therefore an important process of research enabling findings from the sample to be seen as typical of the groups being studied and possibly wider society itself.

What are the ethical issues of research?

Given that sociological research involves studying people, it follows that research can have unintended consequences and negatively affect the people who are being researched. It follows, therefore, that researchers have to take into consideration the ethical issues that may derive from their investigation. Therefore, sociologists need to consider the impact their research can have on their respondents and avoid putting themselves in danger by ensuring they conform to professional ethical guidelines such as those published by the British Sociological Association.

Informed consent

Informed consent refers to the freely given consent by respondents to taking part in research. In order for participants to sign their consent, they should be told about the nature and purpose of the research. All participants should always be able to refuse to co-operate and withdraw at any time for the research. Participants in research should always be aware that the researcher is undertaking research, except where covert research is appropriate and justified.

Preserve confidentiality

All data collected should be treated in the strictest confidence and anonymity should be guaranteed to respondents. In order to avoid inadvertently giving away people's identities, their background and characteristics should only be described in a limited way.

Effects on people being studied

It is essential that participants are neither hurt nor disadvantaged by research. That is, researchers should consider the consequences of their investigation and ensure that no-one is adversely affected psychologically, physically or socially. This is particularly likely to happen when researching sensitive issues where people are vulnerable, such as attempted suicide, victims of violence, eating disorders, etc. Where research builds up 'close relationships' then sociologists should exercise their professional judgement to ensure their practice is correct and appropriate.

Competence

All sociologists should embark upon research in a professional manner that does not bring the subject into disrepute. In addition, researchers must take care to avoid situations that involve breaking the law or engaging in inappropriate behaviour. Finally, sociologists should consider any consequences or misuse that could be made of their work once published, however unintentional.

Grade boost

Remember to discuss ethical issues, with examples if possible, when answering research methods questions in exams. Examiners will reward an awareness of ethical problems, especially when supported with research evidence. Using textbooks and your class notes, use the blank spaces in this book to add research studies.

Researchers should always get informed consent from respondents.

quickfire

③ Why should researchers be wary of researching sensitive issues even when respondents seem willing?

Key figure

Laud Humphreys undertook an infamous and ethically dubious observation study of homosexual men in public toilets in the USA (*Tearoom Trade*, 1970).

Key Terms

Going native = when sociologists lose their academic detachment by getting too close to the group they are studying.

Grade boost

Practical issues are often overlooked by candidates in exam answers about research methods. It is important that they are discussed in a more detailed manner than a quick reference to 'problems of time and money'.

quickfire

④ Why do you think the government makes researchers sign a 'gagging' contract?

Key figure

Paul Willis (1977) undertook classic participant observation study in a Midlands comprehensive school. To overcome the practical problem of gaining access to and building a rapport with school pupils he worked initially in the school coffee shop.

What practical problems are associated with research?

Sociological research, in addition to theoretical and ethical issues, also comes up against some practical problems. These can sometimes make or break a piece of research and play a major role in determining whether research is successful or not.

Financial

Research is expensive, especially if it takes place over a long period of time and involves a team rather than an individual researcher. Clearly, without adequate funding, planned research cannot take place. However, there are additional issues such as the source providing the funding having a prior agenda or preconceived ideas about what findings it expects from the research. The largest provider of research funds in the UK is the government, but in return all sociologists sign a contract that can restrict the publication of anything that does not reflect the government's values.

Time

Research can be very time consuming which adds to its expense. With longitudinal research, projects can be terminated prematurely because of either lack of funds or the participants dropping out as they lose interest with the project.

Researchers' careers

All research-based sociologists are interested in achieving a successful career. They are under pressure from their academic establishments to publish books and research papers. Research choice is rarely a free choice, influenced by factors like what is their specialist area, what research might lead to promotion or what area of research is most likely to attract funding. Finally, the relationship to the aims of the study can be a factor, for example whether it is a qualitative or quantitative approach.

Choice of method

The research situation often dictates which method would be most appropriate. For example, the only practical method of researching a large number of people is through questionnaires. So sometimes researchers are forced to use methods they are not necessarily comfortable with.

Proximity to respondents

Sociologists use the phrase '**going native**' to describe the situation when researchers get very close to their respondents so that they effectively become one of them. This can be a good thing, in the sense of gaining very valid data, but it can also stop researchers thinking objectively and recording data appropriately. Where research involves different groups, siding with one can cause other groups to distance themselves from the researcher or lead to conflict.

What is meant by sampling?

The **target population** of any research is the group being studied, which can often be very large, sometimes many millions of people. Because it would be impractical to approach every person in the target population, a representative sample is used. This sample is drawn from a representative list of people within the target population, known as the **sampling frame**. Examples of sampling frames include electoral rolls, postcode areas, The Post Office General Address File. Those researched through sampling therefore represent everyone in the target population and providing they are representative should derive the same results as if every member of the target population was researched.

Random sampling

This is the simplest form of sample where everyone in the sampling frame has an equal chance of being drawn and included in the research. A clear drawback of this sample is that if it is too small then it may be unrepresentative, that is, not reflect the characteristics of the target population. A way of ensuring against this is to use stratified random sampling.

Stratified random sampling

This sample is more complex than random sampling and involves a random group drawn from different categories of people in the target population. In this way groups or strata (layers within society such as age, gender or ethnic background) can be brought into the sample in a way that is representative of the target population.

Quota sampling

This is similar to random stratified sampling and involves setting a quota from within pre-selected categories (gender, ethnicity, age, etc.). However, some categories such as social class are not necessarily clearly defined or visible.

Systematic sampling

This involves adding people from a sampling frame at regular intervals such as every fifth name on a register. Like random sampling, if the sample size is small, it may not be representative.

Snowball sampling

When sociologists are researching groups that are hard to access they often use this type of sample. They often start with just one contact and through them gain contact to others. This sample is often, but not necessarily, associated with researching deviant groups like drug-takers, gang members, etc. When sample sizes are small there is a danger of samples being unrepresentative.

Key Terms

Sampling frame = list from which samples are chosen.

Target population = the group being studied in research.

Grade boost

It is important to read exam questions on sampling carefully. They often require you to justify why some samples are more appropriate than others in conducting research. Simply describing different types of sample is not addressing the requirements of such questions.

quickfire

⑤ Why are many types of sample not representative?

Key figure

Goldthorpe *et al.* in their classic *Affluent Worker Study* (1964) deliberately used a non-representative 'purposive sample' drawn from skilled workers in Luton to test if the working class were becoming more like the middle class. They felt conditions were so fertile for finding it there, that if they failed to find it they could safely conclude it didn't exist anywhere in Britain.

Key Terms

Closed questions = where respondents are given a choice of answers.

Open questions = where respondents can elaborate and develop their answers.

Grade boost

In examination answers, when discussing using questionnaires, recognise that whilst most social surveys represent a 'snap-shot' study of a group at a moment in time, there are also longitudinal surveys, which monitor a group over a period of years.

quickfire

⑥ Why might a researcher use a postal questionnaire (or equivalent electronic version)?

Key figure

Nicola Charles in *Social Change, Family Formation and Kin Relationships* (2005) used questionnaires to collect quantitative data in her follow-up study of Rosser and Harris's 1965 classic study of family change conducted in Swansea (*The Family and Social Change*).

Many questionnaires use closed questions.

Why do Sociologists use questionnaires?

Questionnaires are a series of questions, either on paper or electronic forms, for respondents to answer in their own writing (or by typing and clicking boxes). Using questionnaires is the commonest way of collecting data in social surveys. Questionnaires are versatile and can be distributed directly to a group, sent through the post, emailed to respondents or placed on a web page. The feminist Sheer Hite included her questionnaire in women's magazines in order to gain a voluntary sample of female respondents' sexual experiences.

Characteristics of questionnaires

Questionnaires are generally compiled from **closed questions** and consequently yield quantitative data that can be quickly scanned, analysed and presented as statistics or graphically. Questionnaires are seen to generate data that tends to be quite high in reliability. Although it is possible to ask **open questions**, questionnaires are less useful for collecting qualitative data. As a method they are seen as being lower in validity, compared to unstructured interviews or observation.

Advantages of questionnaires

Some textbooks imply that questionnaires are only used by positivists because of their association with quantitative data. However, any researcher can use questionnaires, especially if they have a large number of respondents or the sample is dispersed over a wide geographical area. Another benefit of questionnaires is that they are less time consuming and relatively cheap to administer as no interviewers are required. Another benefit here is that there are reduced demand characteristics as there is no risk of an interviewer effect or interviewer bias. Because questionnaires are typically completed in privacy and often offer anonymity, it is argued that they offer a useful method for asking sensitive or personal questions.

Disadvantages of questionnaires

The response rate from questionnaires is notoriously low, particularly with postal or emailed questionnaires. This has implications for the representativeness of those who make the effort to respond. With handwritten responses there is invariably a problem with incomplete, illegible or deliberately incorrect answers. Whereas interviewers can judge if people are telling the truth and explain ambiguous or confusing questions, with questionnaires respondents may not understand some questions. Questionnaires may be viewed as an inflexible method, as there is no opportunity to probe interesting answers or observe the social context in which questions were answered. Finally, although high in reliability, questionnaires tend to be low in validity.

Why do Sociologists use interviews?

Interviews involve asking people questions, usually in a one-to-one situation but can also take the form of group interviews and focus groups. In practical terms interviews can be structured (formal), **semi-structured** and unstructured (informal). The former is effectively an interviewer reading out a questionnaire and writing down the answers, the latter is essentially a conversation perhaps with some common questions as ice-breakers and to help build up a good relationship between interviewer and interviewee.

Characteristics of interviews

Interviews are a method favoured by interpretive sociologists, because apart from structured interviews, they tend to use open questions which yield qualitative data. Interviews are therefore seen to generate data that tends to be quite high in validity. However, as a method they are seen as being lower in reliability compared to questionnaires.

Structured interviews

Transcribing answers is not normally a problem with structured interviews as the questions are of a closed nature, often multiple-choice. Positivists view structured interviews as scientific because they are standardised, reliable and generate quantifiable results.

Unstructured interviews

Informal interviews are favoured by interpretive sociologists as they typically yield qualitative data that is rich in validity. They are informal sessions involving the interviewer asking open-ended questions about a topic. Respondents are encouraged to answer freely and in depth.

Advantages of interviews

Compared to questionnaires the response rate tends to be higher. Interviewers are in a position to clarify terms or explain ambiguous questions. In addition, if an interviewer can observe facial expression, tone of voice, body language, and there is suspicion that a respondent is lying then their answers can be discarded.

Disadvantages of interviews

Interviews are more time consuming and expensive than questionnaires. In addition, unstructured interviews require expensive and time-consuming training as successful research depends on the skills of the interviewer. There is always the danger of an 'interviewer effect' whereby their presence can influence the responses given. The small size of samples can undermine their representativeness and thus make generalisations difficult.

Key Terms

Rapport = the good relationship between interviewer and interviewee.

Semi-structured interviews = a cross between structured and unstructured interviews. There may be common questions but supplementary questions may occur in response to answers.

Grade boost

When writing about interviews in exam answers, don't forget the example of focus groups where a group is invited to discuss their views on an issue raised by the researcher. As a method it shares a lot of characteristics with unstructured interviews.

quickfire

(7) What type of sociologists favour using semi-structured and unstructured interviews?

Key figure

Caroline Gatrell used in-depth unstructured interviews to collect qualitative data on the experiences of working mothers in her book *Hard Labour* (2004). Interestingly, in terms of sampling she adopted a snowballing approach where one participant introduced another.

Ethnography = literally means the study of people, but a term used synonymously for participant observation.

Overt research = where a researcher is openly observing a group with their knowledge.

Covert research = where a group is being studied but they are unaware of this.

Grade boost

When writing about observation in an exam answer, besides talking about qualitative and valid data and that it is a method favoured most by interactionists, remember it can be used by other sociologists such as the Marxist Paul Willis in his study of 'lads' in *Learning to Labour* (1977).

 **quickfire**

⑧ What does the term 'going native' mean?

Key figure

Simon Winlow (*Badfellas: Crime Tradition and New Masculinities*, 2001) used an **ethnographic** approach of participant observation of bouncers in Sunderland by working as a bouncer himself in clubs and pubs for over four years.

Why do Sociologists use observation?

Observation is a method favoured by interpretive sociologists as a means of collecting qualitative data that is high in validity. This is because people are observed going about everyday routines within a natural setting. However, because observation is almost impossible to replicate, it is low in reliability. Observation can be:

- Overt non-participant (*those observed are aware they are being studied*)
- Covert non-participant (*those observed are unaware they are being studied*)
- Overt participant (*researcher participates amongst those observed in an open way whereby they aware they are being studied*)
- Covert participant (*researcher participates amongst those observed in a hidden way so that they are unaware that they are being studied*)

Overt observation

The problem with **overt research** is that if people are aware they are being studied, they no longer behave normally or naturally. This is known as the 'observer effect', which is a form of the Hawthorne effect.

Covert observation

It is felt that because people are unaware of being studied, their behaviour is natural. It is often, but not necessarily, adopted when groups are involved in deviant behaviour such as the study of gangs. **Covert research** raises ethical concerns about spying on people, but is justified in terms of the naturalistic nature of the research yielding valid qualitative data.

Advantages of observation

Observation tends to produce qualitative data rich in validity. It often takes place over a long period of time, allowing the researcher to really get to know the group being studied. Because the researcher blends into the background and people are presumably behaving naturally, it leads to valid data. Sometimes, as William F. Whyte noted, you can learn the unexpected, such as answers to the questions researchers would not have thought to ask.

Disadvantages of observation

Observation tends to be low in reliability as there is little chance of replicating the study. In addition, researchers have to guard against 'going native', whereby they become so close to the group that there is a danger their observations become biased and subjective. Because observations take place over a long period of time, they are both time consuming and costly. The ethical issues of covert observation led to the British Sociological Association discouraging their use.

Why do Sociologists use other secondary sources?

Both positivist and interpretive sociologists can use secondary data which have been collected and published by someone else. However, the source and authenticity of secondary data is very important in order to check that it is not **biased** or **over-subjective**. Official documents and statistics tend to yield quantitative data, whereas letters, diaries and oral histories tend to provide qualitative data.

Previous sociological research

Most sociologists will begin their research with a literature search of existing data on the topic area they plan to study. This prevents wasteful duplication, and prior research can help formulate the direction of study or the composition of research questions.

Documents

Sociologists use the term 'document' to include historical documents (parish records, census data, etc.) as well as personal documents (diaries and letters). Whereas in the past these would invariably be paper-based, today documents can include electronic data as well as audio and video recordings. With any document it can be difficult to evaluate its accuracy or validity or to establish just how representative the content is.

Media sources

The mass media is a major source of both quantitative and qualitative data. For example, the work by the Glasgow University Media Group has centred on a **formal content analysis** of television news on issues like the portrayal of strikes, the Gulf War and coverage of AIDS.

Advantages of secondary sources

The data already exists and is usually readily and cheaply available in an accessible form (often electronically). Historical documents help put research into a historical context. Sometimes practical reasons necessitate the use of secondary sources. For example, geographical distance or a researcher does not participate in research; perhaps of illegal behaviour, deviant or dangerous people.

Disadvantages of secondary sources

Researchers often have no idea of how secondary data was obtained so cannot guarantee it was collected in a rigorous and systematic fashion. Secondary data can also contain personal biases, errors or be incomplete, making generalisations difficult. Some concepts or terms may be **operationalised** in a strange or different way.

Key Terms

Formal content analysis = the systematic study of text, pictures or symbols.

Operationalisation = the translation of a concept or term into an understandable form. For example, when discussing religiosity, the researcher has to explain what is meant by this: publicly practising a religion, believing in some God or having spiritual beliefs.

Bias = when the personal opinions or values of the researcher influence their findings.

Over-subjective = when research loses its objectivity and reflects the personal values of researcher.

Grade boost

When writing about secondary sources and data, break down your answer into the benefits and pitfalls of its use, supplementing your answer with examples.

quickfire

⑨ Why should secondary sources be used with caution?

Key figure

Phillip Aries used old oil paintings as evidence to support his research into the social construction of childhood for his book *Centuries of Childhood* (1960).

Key Terms

Census = a count of the population every ten years that also asks questions about behaviour and attitudes.

British Crime Survey = a national victim survey that asks around 40,000 households about their experiences as victims of crime in the past 12 months.

Grade boost

To add sociological depth to your exam answer on official statistics include analysis of how different perspectives (Interactionism, Marxism, Feminism, etc.) view official statistics.

⊙ quickfire

(10) Why do sociologists use official statistics?

Key figure

The Sutton Trust (2005) used a range of sources including official statistics to find out the educational background of politicians in their study *The Educational Background of Members of the House of Commons and House of Lords.*

Why do Sociologists use official statistics?

Official statistics reflect the considerable data collected by government departments and agencies. There is an abundance of official statistics about all areas of society. Being readily available, generally up to date and often free, they are an important source of data for sociologists. There are some official statistics that are described as 'complete' because they are extremely accurate, such as birth, death, marriage and divorce rates. However, many sociologists view other official statistics as little more than a social construction. Some official statistics are consequently more useful than others.

Benefits of official statistics

Official statistics are regularly updated allowing trends over time to be monitored. They are often based on large samples so are representative. For example, the **Census** collects data on the total population of 64 million and the **British Crime Survey** is based on a sample of 40,000 households. For sociologists, official statistics can provide useful background material to research, which in turn can provide supporting evidence or useful insights into their research.

Problems with official statistics

Because they are created by government and its agencies, sociologists have no control over what methods were used to gather them. Often this means that making comparisons is difficult, as official definitions may not match those of the sociologist. Many sociologists question the accuracy of statistics and talk about a 'dark figure' of unrecorded data in official statistics (such as unrecorded crime, unemployment, suicide, etc.).

Sociological perspectives and official statistics

Interpretive sociologists argue that official statistics should always be used critically as they question the authenticity and reliability of statistics. With the exception of some official statistics such as birth rates, marriage rates, death rates, etc., which are very reliable, they argue that most official statistics are social constructions. Marxists focus on the ideological role of official statistics, arguing that the data is often manipulated for political reasons; for example, unemployment defined in such a way that it minimises its size. Feminists also challenge the ideological and sexist assumptions that can underpin official statistics, such as assuming the head of a household is automatically male.

Research Methods: Summary

We have identified the key points of this topic on the WJEC AS specification, i.e. the bare minimum you need to know. You may want to fill in further details to elaborate and personalise this content.

Positivist approach

1. Collects quantitative data in form of statistics
2. Seeks objective 'social facts'
3. Looks to find correlations between social phenomena
4. Ultimate goal is 'cause and effect' relationships

Realist approach

Has qualities taken from both of these approaches and collects quantitative and qualitative data

Interpretive approach

- Collects qualitative data from people-centred research
- Sees reality as subjective
- Emphasis upon interpretation and people-centred research
- Because humans have consciousness, we should give meaning to their actions

Methods typically used

- Questionnaires
- Structured interviews

Types of sample

- Random
- Stratified
- Quota
- Systematic
- Snowball

Methods typically used

- Semi-structured interviews
- Unstructured interviews
- Observation

Qualities

- High in reliability, low in validity

Secondary data

- Official statistics
- Personal documents
- Historical documents
- Media sources

Qualities

- High in validity, low in reliability

Ethical issues

- Informed consent
- Anonymity and confidentiality
- No-one should be harmed
- Researchers should be honest about purpose of research
- Debriefing after research
- No laws should be broken

Practical issues

- Financial
- Time and resources needed
- Researcher's career
- Methods to be used
- Proximity to respondents

Important considerations

Is the research biased or value-laden in any way? Is the sample representative?
Can generalisations be made from the findings of the research?

SY2 Education

When revising education, focus on the main debates and issues. For example, the specification notes that education is an agency of social control, so you may be asked questions about the role of education as an agency of socialisation. In addition, although education can be a route to better life chances for some students, it may act as a negative factor for others. Some people will fail to achieve their potential because they lack qualifications in a society which values education. More importantly, entire social groups, such as members of ethnic minorities and members of some social classes, may be disadvantaged for reasons beyond their control. Reasons for these inequalities may lie in the home or in the education system itself.

Revision checklist

Tick column 1 when you have completed brief revision notes.
Tick column 2 when you think you have a good grasp of the topic.
Tick column 3 during final revision when you feel you have mastery of the topic.

		1	2	3
p60 **Why do we educate children?**	Formal and informal education			
	Formal education in the UK			
	Theories of education			
p61 **History of education (1960s to the present day)**	Comprehensive schools			
	Conservatism and the marketisation of education			
	Tony Blair and New Labour			
	David Cameron and the Coalition			
p62 **Key legislation in education since the 1960s**	1960s–1979			
	1979–1997			
	1997–2010			
	2010–			
p63 **Types of school in the UK**	Types of school			
	Independent schools			
p64 **Structural theories of education**	Functional theories of education			
	Conflict theories of education			
p65 **Labelling theory and social interactionism**	Stereotyping			
	Self-fulfilling prophecy			

			1	2	3
p66	**Patterns of educational attainment**	Social class			
		Gender			
		Ethnicity			
p67	**Cultural deprivation and school attainment**	Cultural deprivation			
		Underclass theory			
		Cultural capital			
p68	**Material deprivation and school attainment**	The extent of material deprivation			
		Financial disadvantage at school			
		Social disadvantage and school			
		Intellectual disadvantage			
p69	**Factors within schools that contribute to pupil failure**	Labelling theory and social class			
		Gender issues			
		Ethnicity			
		School effectiveness			
p70	**Factors in society that impact on educational success**	Political intervention			
		Funding differences			
		Private education			

Key Terms

Social placement = children are trained to accept their future roles in society.

Informal education = education that takes place in the family or through normal life.

Formal education = education that is institutionalised, with trained teachers, exams and a set curriculum.

Grade boost

Although education is compulsory between the ages of 5 and 16 in the UK; it is not necessary for children to attend school if their parents can satisfy assessors that they are qualified to educate their children.

quickfire

① Why do we need schools to educate our children in the UK?

Key figure

Marshall (1998) pointed out that modern societies operate a system of credentialism. This means that people require increasing numbers of formal qualifications to prove they are suitable for jobs. Qualifications act as a form of social selection, so unqualified people become unemployable.

Why do we educate children?

Formal and informal education

Many societies have no **formal education** system and children are not expected to attend schools. Children learn what they need to know from the adults around them. This is known as **informal education**.

In most developed countries, education is compulsory and children must be educated by law. This process usually takes place in institutions whose responsibility is to educate children; schools and colleges. Education that takes place in institutional settings is known as formal education. There is a plan of learning, trained teachers and a formal assessment process.

Formal education in the UK

Until the 1870 Education Act in the UK, only rich children, and usually just boys, would have had an education. Often it was the church or charitable institutions that provided basic schooling. The terms of the Act meant that all children between the ages of 5 and 12 were expected to attend schools. Most education Acts have increased the amount of compulsory education that children are expected to receive.

Education is an agency of socialisation. The introduction of formal education in a society is usually prompted by political, economic or social needs. These may include educating people into the basic skills needed to be a good workforce or to educate them into military training. Education acts as a form of child protection, so children cannot be forced to work in factories or farms. Education is also a form of social control, so children are taught basic social conduct. In many cultures, education has been provided as part of a religious training. In modern societies, education has a role as **social placement**. Children are identified and then trained for future roles or work in society.

Increasingly, educational success is the best route to a good job.

Theories of education

- Durkheim believed education was important as it transmits the core values of society to children.
- Parsons suggested we need schools to build a bridge between family life and the wider world.
- Marxists claim that schools act to train children into capitalism where they learn to accept social inequalities as natural and fair.

History of education (1960s to the present day)

In the 1960s, most children between the ages of 11 and 15 attended **selective schools**. In theory, the gifted attended grammar schools, in practice, these schools were middle-class institutions and many able working-class children attended schools where they could only gain low value qualifications if they were even entered for exams.

Comprehensive schools

The Labour government (1964–1970) attempted to introduce **comprehensive schools** where all children could have access to the same curriculum. This policy was not particularly successful. Many of the new schools still had selective classes. There was a feeling that education in the UK was failing. This was 'the Great Debate', prompted by a speech from Prime Minister Callaghan.

Conservatism and the marketisation of education

Margaret Thatcher (Prime Minister 1979–1990) was elected on the basis of a belief in leaving the economy to solve society's problems. She wanted schools to run like businesses, so parents could choose which schools to send their children to. Schools had to compete in a market for the best pupils. Her government introduced the National Curriculum, changed teacher training and reduced the power of councils to control schools and plan education. She also introduced fees for universities. There were eleven Education Acts in her term of office. John Major (1990–1997) pursued similar policies encouraging new forms of schools to be developed, such as City Technology colleges.

Tony Blair and New Labour

New Labour (1997–2007) disappointed many people because it continued with New Right policies. It continued to encourage competition between schools. Different types of school such as City Academies were set up; the government gave money to the Church of England to create schools. The Blair Government increased spending on education, and results appeared to improve. However, the focus of legislation was to encourage selection in schools, place schools and teachers under pressure from external agencies such as Ofsted, change the examination system and encourage the more traditional education that benefits the wealthy.

David Cameron and the Coalition

With the election only taking place in 2010, it is difficult to predict events. However, the indications are that this government will attempt to **privatise** education still further and return to a traditional curriculum. Tuition fees in universities have already been raised and EMA abolished in England.

Key Terms

Selective schools = the school is able to choose which pupils are allowed to attend. This is done on ability to pass examinations.

Comprehensive schools = all children have equal access to the curriculum.

Privatise = remove government economic control from an industry or agency.

Grade boost

Some detailed knowledge of major Education Reform Acts is useful, but you should also be aware of how the Acts have influenced the education system and the way that pupils experience school.

quickfire

② Create a time line of how schools have changed since the 1960s.

Key figures

Chitty and Dunford (1999) and **Mortimore** (2007) said that the best performing countries in education had a system of fully comprehensive schools that were controlled democratically by local communities and where teachers were respected by government and the population.

Key Terms

Specialist colleges = schools raise sponsorship and in return get additional government funding and the right to select pupils.

National Curriculum = the set of knowledge and skills that all schools should pass on to pupils; some schools are exempt from this: private schools.

City academies = privately run schools paid for by the state.

Grade boost

The present day system of education in the UK is complex, with a variety of different school types and systems of funding. This is as a result of a series of educational reports, circulars and Acts of Parliament, most of which have removed power from Local Education Authorities and given powers to central government.

quickfire

(3) Suggest reasons why governments are so concerned with creating legislation that reforms or changes the education system and schools.

Key figure

Ivan Illich (1971) was an influential thinker of the 1970s. He was critical of formal education systems and suggested that they be replaced by skill centres and information exchanges so individuals could follow up on their special interests.

Key legislation in education since the 1960s

1965 Circular 10/65 advised all education authorities to plan comprehensive schools in their areas.

1969–1977 Five **Black Papers** (pamphlets) were issued by Conservative thinkers arguing for choice, competition and parental control of schools.

1979 Education Act gave schools the right to select pupils.

1980 Education Act gave parents more rights over schools and established the Assisted Places Scheme, which sent poorer pupils to expensive private schools.

1986 Education (No. 2) Act gave governing bodies powers over schools and head teachers.

1988 Education Reform Act (the Baker Act) imposed the National Curriculum, introduced Assessment Tests for children at 7, 11, 14 and 16, gave control over school finance to governing bodies and made schools open to market forces by setting them in competition with each other for the best pupils.

1990 Education (Student Loans) Act removed grants for university students and established a system of repayable loans.

1992 Education (Schools) Act established inspection bodies Ofsted (England) and Estyn (Wales).

1993 Education Act made the establishment of new schools easier, reduced testing and the content of the **National Curriculum** and established 'special measures' of inspection for schools deemed to be failing.

1998 School Standards and Framework Act increased the abilities of schools to select pupils, insisted all primary schools offer an hour of literacy and an hour of mathematics every day, set targets for school improvements and set up Education Action Zones in deprived areas.

2000 Tony Blair announced comprehensive schools would be turned into '**specialist colleges**'. **City academies** were established.

2002 more faith schools were to be created and supported by government money.

2008 Education and Skills Act raised the school leaving age to 18 from 2015 and gave pupils the right to be consulted on school policy.

2010 Free schools are to be encouraged; they are state-funded schools set up in response to parental demand.

Can you suggest reasons why many parents would choose a single-faith school for their children?

Types of school in the UK

In the UK, schools are funded with public and private money. Some schools are controlled by local authorities but others are controlled by businesses or charities. There are many different forms of school because a succession of governments has followed contradictory policies of allowing both selection of pupils and offering parental choice over the schools their children should attend. The types of schools that you might find in an area depend on where you are in the country. In Wales, for example, many children are educated through the medium of Welsh.

Types of school

State schools are owned by local authorities who allocate money and employ staff. This is probably the most common type of school. These include comprehensive schools, grammar schools, and secondary modern schools.

Foundation schools have more freedom than community schools because the governing body can select pupils and employ staff. These schools may also include comprehensives and grammar schools.

Voluntary-aided schools are owned by charities and they employ staff. They may be religious **faith schools**. City Technology Colleges are independent from Local Authorities, but do not charge fees. They tend to offer vocational qualifications.

City Academies are independent from local authorities with many funded by businesses or charities. Large numbers are linked to religious groups. They were often set up on the sites of failing schools and many offer vocational education. They have been controversial and there is no agreement on their relative success in turning around poor attainment.

Specialist schools have extra funding to establish a centre of excellence in certain subject areas, although they must teach the whole curriculum. There are over 2,600 such schools in England where they are given additional funding if they can be sponsored by business interests.

Independent schools such as Harrow are often historical institutions conferring privilege and status on their pupils.

Independent schools

In some areas you might also find **independent schools** (private schools) that are usually run as businesses and charge fees to parents. There are approximately 2,300 such schools in the country. The most famous and best of these privately owned schools are also called public schools.

Key Terms

Faith schools = these are schools that are organised and run on religious grounds; they were supported by Tony Blair.

Independent schools = these are privately owned and known as private schools; they are run as businesses or as charities. The best schools are called public schools.

Grade boost

It probably isn't necessary to understand the different types of school in much detail, though the City Academy debate is an important one. It is more important to recognise the effect that the complexity of the education system has on the quality of education offered to different social groups in our society.

quickfire

④ What are the advantages and disadvantages of having a variety of different types of schools in our society?

Key figure

Stephen Gorard (2005) claims that government policies act against social mixing in schools. This happens because middle-class people avoid poorly performing schools and select schools that have a record of success. Middle-class drift is where parents move to the catchments of good schools.

Key Terms

Hidden curriculum = that which schools teach without intending to or being aware of what they are teaching, these are usually the hidden values of society.

Ideology = a belief system.

Meritocracy = system where intelligence, ability and effort are rewarded.

Cultural capital = the dominant knowledge of a society; those children who have access to the dominant culture will do better in education.

Correspondence theory = inequalities in school reflect wider inequalities in society.

Grade boost

Functional and conflict theories both offer a very similar view of how the education system works. Functionalists are criticised because they do not recognise that children do not have equal access to educational support and conflict theorists because they do not recognise that schools are a route to better lives for many pupils. Be aware of the strengths and weaknesses of each viewpoint.

quickfire

⑤ Outline similarities and differences between Functionalism and conflict theories of education.

Key figure

Pierre Bourdieu (1964) developed the concept of **cultural capital**. He said that schools teach the culture of the dominant social groups in society and those children who have most access to the dominant culture will have a better experience and are more likely to succeed in school.

Structural theories of education

Structural theories of society look at the way society is organised and how the institutions of society affect people.

Functional theories of education

Functionalism is based on the theory that societies are held together by consensus. People share values which they learn through a process of socialisation. The education system is an important way for society to train its new members into the shared knowledge and morality of a culture. Durkheim believed that children learn the attitudes that they will require to survive as adults through the school system because this is an orderly and regulated environment.

In addition, schools and education act as a form of social selection whereby the best students are prepared for the most important and best paid jobs in society. Munro and also Davie and Moore suggest that those students who prove that they do not have the character and aptitude for the better positions learn that they will do the least intellectually demanding and lowest paid work. Parsons believed that one of the most important roles of a school is to identify some children as failures in order that others could be seen as successful. Functionalists believe this is **meritocracy**.

Conflict theories of education

Marxists and Feminists believe that society is composed of different groups who are in competition for power. Schools exist to reinforce the dominant power systems and train children through the workings of the **hidden curriculum** to accept inequality as being normal and correct. Bowles and Gintis (1976) suggested that schools reflect the wider inequality of society; this is **correspondence theory**.

The education system passes on **ideology**, the dominant ideology being that of the most powerful groups in society. For Marxists, the dominant ideology is that of wealthy people; for Feminists, it is the ideology of gender divisions. Louis Althusser, a Marxist, believed that schools are part of the ideological state apparatus of society, existing to control children's minds. Olin Wright, a Neo-Marxist, says that schools promote policies of equality, but in reality, their practice reflects the major inequalities that exist in society.

Labelling theory and social interactionism

Labelling theory originated in the USA, as a response to and criticism of Functionalism. It is concerned with the way in which individuals develop a sense of identity from their interactions with other people, and the ways in which other people respond to them.

Stereotyping

People have a general tendency to categorise others in a simplistic way. These categories are known as **stereotypes**. They may be based on simple beliefs and impressions, but they influence how we treat others.

If someone fits into a positive stereotype, for example, is attractive, clean and neat, then others may overlook negative aspects of their personality. This is known as the halo effect. However, if someone fits a negative stereotype, for example by being a member of a particular ethnic group or being disabled, then more positive aspects of their personalities are ignored.

Thus, a child may fit a teacher's stereotype and then be labelled as 'good' or 'bad' by teaching staff before education even begins. Nell Keddie (1970) argued that many teachers have an image of an ideal student in their minds, and generally, this is a middle-class child. Thus working-class children may be disadvantaged.

Labelling theorists point out that teachers often have a stereotype of a perfect pupil and favour those who fit this image over more challenging students.

Self-fulfilling prophecy

This is the belief that behaviour can be reinforced by the imposition of a label. If children are given a negative label, then they may either accept or reject the label. If they accept the label, they will believe themselves to be 'bad' students and then react by behaving in a negative fashion in school.

Hargreaves (1975) found that children who were placed in lower sets or streams in schools became rejecting of school and education. He further pointed out that working-class children were more likely to be labelled as being of lower ability. Teachers would be critical of the behaviour of lower sets; the pupils would then behave in a way that reinforced the label. This resulted in academic underachievement. However, Safia Mirza (1992) found that ethnic minority pupils resisted labels and worked for educational success despite negative teacher labelling.

Key Terms

Labelling = a process whereby people assume knowledge about others and then behave as though that knowledge were true.

Stereotype = a way of categorising people based on exaggerated, generalised and simplistic assumptions of a group's characteristics.

Self-fulfilling prophecy = people often behave in the way they are expected to because of their labels.

Resistance = a Marxist idea, it describes the way that people reject traditional social values of the middle classes and invent their own cultural ideas.

Grade boost

Labelling theory is often criticised because it does not explain how the negative labels come to be applied in the first place and seems to blame teachers for pupils' bad behaviour.

quickfire

(6) List the differences between structural theories of education and labelling theory.

Key figures

Rosenthal and Jacobson (1968) conducted a controversial study where they claimed to offer proof that a positive label affected the educational outcome for some pupils. Despite the poor quality of the evidence, this was very influential in educational literature.

Patterns of educational attainment

As measured by examination success, different groups of people achieve different results from education. This is an important measure of equality and opportunity in our society, because educational success is linked to adult occupation and future life chances.

Social class

This is the single most significant factor affecting a child's educational attainment. Aldridge (2001) says that evidence suggests that among children with the same measured intelligence, middle-class children experience more success in school than working-class children. This is a pattern that has changed little despite sixty years of government legislation and control of schools in order to improve standards. Government statistics show that children eligible for free school meals are half as likely to achieve acceptable standards in literacy and numeracy. They are less likely to attend university and few attend top universities.

Gender

Until the 1970s, males were the gender of success. Girls were not expected or required to achieve well in school. Changes in the curriculum and in society have meant that girls are now achieving better than boys at GCSE and A level and more go to university. Within universities, males tend to achieve higher than women, but this pattern is beginning to change as well. Helen Wilkinson (1994) termed this fundamental shift in society, the '**genderquake**'. Both genders are improving, but girls are improving overall much more quickly than boys. Boys are now the gender of failure and this is seen as a problem for society. Males tend to do better in science and mathematics than languages but girls still tend to achieve higher results in these subjects overall.

Girls' achievement on average is better than that of boys. Is this a matter for concern?

Ethnicity

Patterns of achievement by **ethnicity** are complex. Generally, however, Indian and Chinese heritage children do very well in education, outperforming other ethnicities and white children. In contrast, Bangladeshi and West Indian heritage children underperform. This may be complicated by social class factors, as Indian and Chinese children tend to come from wealthier backgrounds.

Key Terms

Social class = this is a measure based on occupational and educational background with working-class people tending to earn less and have fewer academic qualifications.

Ethnicity = the cultural background with which you identify.

Genderquake = a fundamental shift in social attitudes that mean girls are now the gender of success.

Grade boost

There are many explanations for differences in attainment in school, but intelligence probably is not significant compared to the social factors of class, gender and ethnicity. The reasons for differences in attainment may be related to poverty and deprivation or to factors within schools. The worst achieving groups are white working-class boys.

quickfire

⑦ Why is success in school important in our society?

Key figures

Official statistics are collected by a number of government bodies and the range and variety of educational statistics has deepened as governments have set targets for success by schools. These can be seen online; they have the advantage of being very reliable but there may be questions about their validity.

Cultural deprivation and school attainment

There are cultural differences between the social classes. However, these are difficult to measure or quantify. Theories from both functionalist and Marxist perspectives have said that cultural differences may affect attainment but they differ in how the process is said to work.

Cultural deprivation

Some functionalists and others have claimed that the culture of working-class people is somehow worse or antagonistic towards schools. Recently, writers such as Melanie Phillips and Sue Palmer have suggested that working-class people are not good at parenting. They transmit values that cause children to fail in school. This is not a new idea. In the 1950s, Lewis described a 'culture of poverty' that helped poor people to survive, but which also led to failure. In the 1970s, Basil Bernstein claimed that middle-class people are able to use language in a different way from working-class people; working-class people are thus limited when they attend school as schools rely on middle-class culture. Brown (1987) found that high achieving pupils in working-class schools are bullied. Despite these ideas being heavily criticised, they still persist and policy makers rely on them to explain school failure.

Underclass theory

New Right thinkers such as Charles Murray (1996) suggest that the existence of the welfare state means that some people have come to rely on benefits to survive. They have no ambition for their children and allow them to fail in school or even undermine education. Despite the evidence for this being weak, it has been influential in determining government policy.

Understanding of high culture such as opera and ballet may give middle-class students an advantage in education.

Cultural capital

Marxists tend to look at the fit between middle-class school culture and working-class culture. Bourdieu developed the idea that the middle classes have access to cultural capital. This is knowledge of how the system works and information about culture itself. Middle-class people set the curriculum. This puts working-class people at a disadvantage. There is strong supporting evidence for this view. Ball *et al.* (1995) found middle-class parents were able to talk to teachers better and Gillies (2005) found middle-class parents develop a range of strategies to gain advantage for their children.

Key Terms

Underclass = a group of people at the bottom of society who rely on benefits and choose not to work.

Cultural capital = the background knowledge that one requires to gain success and attainment in school.

Cultural deprivation = the idea that working-class children fail because their values are inferior to those of middle-class children.

Grade boost

It is very difficult to 'prove' that working-class people and middle-class people have a different culture. Evidence seems to suggest that both groups are equally anxious for their children to succeed in school. It may be possible that middle-class people have a better understanding of how to achieve their aims for their children.

quickfire

(8) What are the differences between middle-class and working-class culture?

Key figure

Robin Nash (1972) used both labelling theory and the concept of cultural capital. He argued that teachers have individual cultural biases towards some pupils. Pupils need to know how to conform to the teacher's perception of a 'good' student.

Key Terms

Material deprivation = lack of the things necessary for life.

Poverty = the inability to afford the necessary things.

Children who live in cramped accommodation may lack safe places to play; this can affect their physical and mental development.

Grade boost

In examination answers on this topic, candidates sometimes list financial reasons for school failure among poorer students. However, it is wise to remember that material deprivation may have a wider impact on pupils, because they may lack confidence or feel neglected by teaching staff.

quickfire

⑨ Why do children who experience poverty tend to underachieve in school?

Key figure

J W B Douglas (1964) believed that poorer parents showed less interest in schools than richer parents. In addition, he believed that the very able would benefit from education regardless of income. It was middle ability children who were most likely to be negatively affected by low parental income.

Material deprivation and school attainment

Material deprivation refers to **poverty**; it is the lack of things that people require to succeed. In the UK, children who are poor tend to underachieve in school. Much of research into poverty is dated, because until the 1970s, opening opportunities to the able working class was a priority. Later governments were more interested in looking at issues within schools to explain working-class underachievement.

The extent of material deprivation

Government data suggests that 4 million children (30 per cent) are living in poverty in the UK; the proportion of children living in poverty is growing. Spending cuts in the Coalition government (2010) mean poverty rates may rise.

Financial disadvantage at school

Wikeley (2007) found that poorer children had less access to out-of-school activities such as clubs and school trips. Children would not take notes about trips home to avoid pressurising parents. Horgan (2007) found that poorer children were very aware of the cost of things they needed and developed strategies such as truanting on own clothes days to avoid asking for money. Schools created institutional problems for parents: expensive uniform items, after-school meetings that require bus fares, materials for subjects such as art and the need for computer access. Some schools made free school meal provision embarrassing for pupils.

Social disadvantage and school

Better schools can select their pupils; many of the highest attaining will avoid taking on those from low income backgrounds, because problems of social disadvantage sometimes result in behavioural difficulties. Poorer children are vulnerable to bullying and being seen as different (Willow, 2001). They are also more likely to have low attendance. Horgan (2007) found disadvantaged boys to be negative about education from an early age.

Intellectual disadvantage

Feinstein (2003) discovered that intellectual differences on the basis of income can appear in children before they attend school. He suggests a combination of parenting styles and poverty need to be investigated. In addition, he recommends investment in disadvantaged families before children reach school, and investment in schools that serve deprived areas.

Factors within schools that contribute to pupil failure

Much early sociology was concerned with labelling theory and the impact of teacher–pupil relationships on how well pupils were able to achieve. Recent sociology has been concerned with the characteristics of an effective school in order to support government concerns with improving school performance and setting targets.

Labelling theory and social class

Many sociologists worked within schools to investigate why children from working-class backgrounds underachieve. Many sociologists looked at teacher attitudes. They suggested teachers themselves contributed to children's failure and they viewed pupils as the victims. Willis (1977) discovered that working-class boys actively developed a set of attitudes and a subculture which sought failure.

Gender issues

Many feminists undertook work in schools when girls were being failed by the education system. They found sexist reading schemes, a male-orientated curriculum and negative teaching. In 1996, Gordon found teachers to be biased towards boys. Warrington and Younger (2000) found girls choosing stereotypical female subjects that led to low-paid work. Jackson found that laddish cultures developed because of excessive testing and fear of failure. Skidmore (2007) points out that boys are more likely to be excluded and make up 74% of those in specialist behaviour units.

Ethnicity

Sewell (1997) and others have suggested that schools are **racist institutions**. Gillborn and Youdell (2000) claim that some teachers hold 'racialised expectations'. The National Curriculum is **ethnocentric**. Some schools are institutionally racist. Ofsted (2004) found Bangladeshi parents to be ambitious for their children; however, there is a degree of culture clash between schools and parental values. Recently there has been focus on the failure of working-class white pupils compared to ethnic minorities who start with a disadvantage but improve skills in school.

School effectiveness

Pateman (1991), from the New Right, argued that teachers had set agendas for schools, and parents had not been listened to. For example, Sammons *et al.* (1995) found that schools should have effective leadership, good use of resources, continual staff training and safe environments. Blakey and Heath (1992) suggested there was a link between the social class background of the school population and individual school performance.

Key Terms

Ethnocentric = focused on one culture, usually British.

Institutionally racist = the rules and behaviour of the school mean some ethnic groups are treated unfairly or unequally.

School effectiveness = the organisational characteristics that help a school to gain good examination grades for its pupils.

Grade boost

This is a very wide area of research. Much research focuses on the shortcomings of teachers and schools, blaming them for pupil failure to achieve. When evaluating this topic, you may need to consider that pupils are also part of the school and may themselves contribute to their own under-attainment.

quickfire

(10) List the factors within schools that contribute to pupil under-attainment.

Key figure

The Swann Report (1985) claimed schools were partly responsible for the failure of African-Caribbean children because they stereotyped pupils into categories such as 'good at sport' and channelled them into these activities rather than academic success.

Key Term

Public school = privately owned school operating as a charity or as a business.

☐ Excellent
☐ Very good
☐ Good
☐ Average
☑ Poor

Grade boost

When considering reasons for relative school success or failure of certain social groups, it is worth considering whether all children have equal access to the best educational. opportunities. Functionalists tend to overlook these differences between schools but Marxists consider them to be very important.

quickfire

(11) Are all schools in the UK equally good?

Key figure

David Marsh (2002) conducted statistical analysis for private school education of people in power. He noted that both Labour and Conservative cabinets are heavily represented by those who were privately educated and who educate their children privately. Conservative governments tend to have a higher proportion of the privately educated.

Factors in society that impact on educational success

There are a whole range of structural factors that also influence the relative success of pupils. These are to do with how the education system is organised.

Schools in deprived areas of the UK are often seen as 'failing' schools.

Political intervention

Various political processes have contributed to major differences between schools in terms of the achievement of pupils and the quality of provision. The introduction of the idea of competition between schools meant that some schools, usually in middle-class areas, attracted large numbers of able pupils and that other schools then became unpopular and had more pupils with difficulties. It is well known that house prices in the catchment area of good schools are far higher than those in the catchment areas of unpopular schools.

Funding differences

Popular schools have large numbers of pupils and are able to attract larger sums of money for staff and equipment. Smaller, less popular schools have less money. In addition, some school programmes such as the Academies have access to private sponsorship money and new buildings. Faith schools have been given additional funding, and this comes out of the whole budget for education in the UK. There are differences in the regions, too; Wales has less money per pupil than England. Some Local Authorities have less money, or different funding arrangements, so that some schools have limited resources. The schools with more limited resources are often those that attract proportionally larger numbers of pupils with behavioural and learning problems.

Private education

Britain has a large private education sector and upwards of 7 per cent of children are not educated by the state. About 20 per cent of 'A' level students are privately educated. Some schools are poor and have bad facilities, but others are highly privileged with small classes, excellent facilities and access to places at the top universities. Fees may be upwards of £9,000 a year for the top private schools (known as **public schools**). In addition, some of these schools have charitable status, which gives them financial advantages. Wealthy children who attend these schools may have advantages after they leave, because they will have made friends of people who have power and status, which is known as the 'old school-tie network'. Many important politicians and business people in the UK attended public schools.

Education: Summary

We have identified the key points of this topic on the WJEC AS specification, i.e. the bare minimum you need to know. You may want to fill in further details to elaborate and personalise this content.

Patterns of attainment

Why is this important?

Successive British governments have passed legislation to improve education.

Has this legislation been effective?

Despite government intervention in education, patterns of achievement have not altered much.

What is the most important variable affecting school achievement?

Social class is the most significant factor affecting a child's attainment in school.

What other factors affect attainment?

Gender, ethnicity and type of school attended.

What gender patterns can be seen?

Girls were once the underachievers, but are now overtaking boys.

What ethnic patterns are seen?

Some ethnic minorities achieve far better than the majority of white children, but others do significantly worse.

Theories to explain attainment

Functionalists …

…say that schools offer children a ladder of opportunity.

The New Right …

…says that schools are not effective in educating some children and need to compete with each other to improve.

Marxists …

… say that schools act as an agency of social control repressing the working classes.

Feminists …

… say that girls are socialised by the education system to accept lower paid and subordinate positions in society despite their achievements in examinations.

Reasons for working-class under-attainment

Material deprivation

Factors in the home mean that some children do not have the facilities and conditions that they require for success.

Cultural deprivation

Working-class culture is inferior to middle-class culture and children are not trained by their parents to benefit from education.

Social structures

Schools are not equally well funded or well organised, so schools with large numbers of children from deprived backgrounds will struggle for good teachers and motivated students.

Factors within schools

Schools reflect the massive inequalities of society, so they are institutionally racist and sexist, favouring the wealthier students over the poorest.

Cultural capital

Middle-class parents can work systems to favour their own offspring.

SY2 Mass Media

When revising mass media, you should focus on the main debates and issues. For example, you are expected to know the theories of pluralism, Marxism and postmodernism and their application to understanding how the media operates. In addition, you need to understand the arguments and models that examine the relationship between the media and its audience, such as the passive audience models and the active audience models. You may also be asked questions on the nature and change of ownership and control of the media. You should be aware of the impact of both new technology and globalisation on the use of the media. Finally, a common question is to critically discuss the representation of social groups by the media including gender, ethnicity, age and social class.

Revision checklist

Tick column 1 when you have completed brief revision notes.
Tick column 2 when you think you have a good grasp of the topic.
Tick column 3 during final revision when you feel you have mastery of the topic.

			1	2	3
p74	**What are the trends in ownership and control?**	An increasingly global media			
		Integration			
		State media			
		Cybermedia			
		Technological convergence			
		Pluralist approach to media ownership			
		Marxist approach to media ownership			
		Press barons			
p76	**What are news values?**	Pluralism and news values			
		Marxism and news values			
		Neo-Marxism (Hegemonic) and news values			
		Feminism and news values			
		Postmodernism and news values			
p77	**How do the media create moral panics?**	Stan Cohen and mods and rockers			
		Hall *et al.* and mugging			
		Sarah Thornton and rave parties			
		Volatility and short-termism of moral panics			

				1	2	3
p78	**To what extent does the media generate effects on its audience?**	Hypodermic syringe model				
		Active audience models				
		Marxist cultural effects model				
		Postmodernist theory				
p79	**How are new technology and media impacting on the audience?**	Recent trends in new media				
		The digital divide				
p80	**How does globalisation impact upon the media?**	Media via computers				
		Global culture				
		Evaluation of a global media				
p81	**How is gender represented in the media?**	Traditional representations of gender				
		Postmodern representations of gender				
		Media effects and gender				
		Representations of sexuality				
p82	**How is ethnicity represented in the media?**	Portrayal of ethnic minorities as a problem				
		Portrayal of ethnic minorities as a threat				
		Is there scope for optimism?				
p83	**How are class and age represented in the media?**	Does the media reflect a class interest?				
		Representation of class				
		Representation of age				

Grade boost

This is a common examination topic. Prepare yourself for this by having learnt examples of media conglomerates, media barons, and be up to date with changes that are occurring. In addition, supplement your answer with sociological perspective analysis discussed on the next page.

quickfire

① What key global trends are occurring to the mass media?

Key figure

Gillian Doyle (2002) based at Glasgow University's Centre for Cultural Policy Research has highlighted how the concentration of media ownership gives media barons considerable power to influence public opinion through the media.

What are the trends in ownership and control?

The history of the mass media is that ownership is becoming increasingly concentrated as companies take-over and merge with one another. Ben Bagdikian (2004) highlights the rapid concentration of media corporations, currently just seven major ones in the USA: Time-Warner-AOL, Disney (ABC), News Corporation, Sony, Bertelsmann, Viacom (CBS) and General Electric (NBC).

An increasingly global media

Whilst most of these companies are based in the USA, they have become global corporations, dominating the world media market. Thomas McPhail (1981) argues that globalisation has ushered in '**electronic colonialism**' whereby developing countries are subject to '**cultural penetration**' with Western values and culture imposed and swamping their indigenous culture. Many of these multinational corporations are dominated and controlled by one person, for example Rupert Murdoch who owns News Corporation.

Integration

Media companies increase their power, not only by expanding through acquiring similar companies, but by controlling all areas of the media. For example, Murdoch's News Corporation owns newspapers all over the world; including the *Sun* and *Times* in the UK, Fox News, MySpace, HarperCollins books and a major proportion of Sky TV in the UK and Star TV across the bulk of Asia. This pattern is repeated by the seven major global media companies. It enables them to control their operating environment and to engage in **synergy** whereby one area can advertise the other. For example, having put a very expensive satellite into space, Murdoch used his *Sun* newspaper to extensively advertise Sky TV to its readers to build up market share.

State media

In the past, most countries had elements of the media under state control, especially television and radio. Whilst some state broadcasters like the BBC pride themselves on neutrality and objectivity, other countries have had very biased state media; used to defend and prop up unpopular governments. In the UK the BBC had a monopoly over broadcasting up to the 1950s (television) and 1970s (radio). However, like most countries, our media is dominated by commercial media companies, which **pluralists** argue helps promote balance with all points of view being heard. Marxists would question this, arguing that most messages within the media are similar and reflect the commercial interests of their rich owners.

Cybermedia

Sociology textbooks used to talk a lot about the 'press barons' who owned newspapers (see table below). Whilst newspapers are still an important part of the media, their sales are declining. Most newspapers now have a cybermedia presence on the Internet in electronic formats. **Cybermedia** has traditionally been dominated by just four companies: Apple, Microsoft, Google and Yahoo.

Technological convergence

Technological convergence means several technologies can be accessed from just one media product such as email, Internet, maps and mp3 on smartphones, or streaming video and computer games on television sets. Such integration reflects the growth and power of media global conglomerations to search out new areas in order to increase sales and profits.

Pluralist approach to media ownership

Pluralists see the media as a 'window on the world' essentially reflecting back the attitudes and values of the audience. They see the media ownership reflecting, on the one hand, a wide range of views including extreme and minority attitudes, but on the other hand, a broad consensus of public opinion. Pluralists are therefore not over-concerned about media barons, as they argue they largely behave in a responsible manner and have to reflect public opinion in order to sell their media products.

Marxist approach to media ownership

Marxists, like the Glasgow University Media Group, question the diversity of the media, arguing it is essentially made up of bland and mindless content that ideologically serves the rich and powerful who run capitalism. They argue that in order to attract advertising revenue, commercial media have a 'safe' content and generally avoid anything that might annoy or offend. Marxists are also very critical of the power and influence media barons can exert.

Press barons

Rupert Murdoch (News Corporation)	*The Sun, News of the World, The Times, Sunday Times*
Lord Rothermere (Associated Newspapers)	*Daily Mail, Mail on Sunday, Metro, (London's) Evening Standard*
Richard Desmond (United Newspapers)	*Daily Express, Sunday Express, The Star*
Barclay Brothers (Telegraph Group)	*Daily Telegraph, Sunday Telegraph*
Tony O'Reilly	*Independent and Independent on Sunday, Daily Mirror*
Viscount Cowdray (Pearson Group)	*Financial Times*

Key Terms

Cybermedia = media on the Internet.

Technological convergence = the trend for combining several digital media on one media product such as a smartphone.

Grade boost

It is essential that exam answers rise above common-sense answers. One way of adding sociological depth to your answers is to show a good understanding of sociological perspectives and be aware of the contrasts between them.

quickfire

② Why are pluralists unconcerned by media barons?

Key figure

Frankfurt School (1930s onwards) as neo-Marxists they saw the media as a diversionary institution, and talk of 'culture industry' whereby the media create and distribute diversionary cultural goods. By focusing upon trivia and sensationalism, the media helps take people's minds off important issues like poverty, inequality and class oppression.

Churnalism = term coined by Davies to reflect the pressures on modern-day journalists to simply recycle stories produced by spin doctors and PR departments.

Infotainment = process whereby news has been reduced to a combination of 'information' and 'entertainment'.

Hegemonic = process whereby ordinary people are led to believe that the prevailing existing order is somehow natural and normal.

Grade boost

When answering questions on news values, ensure that you bring in factors such as the role of gatekeepers, churnalism, selectivity, personalisation of news stories, cultural factors, gender bias and the demonisation of certain groups as well as sociological perspectives.

quickfire

③ What is meant by churnalism?

Key figure

The Sutton Trust (2006) looked into the educational background of leading journalists and found the majority were educated in private schools. This supports the neo-Marxist hegemonic view that the background of journalists shapes news values.

What are news values?

Pluralism and news values

Pluralists reject the view that the media set the news agenda, seeing the media as a window on the world and therefore reflecting back what the public want. They argue that media professionals know from experience what the public are interested in and what are regarded as important issues. As a neo-pluralist, Nick Davies (2008) sees journalists as 'truth telling' but sees modern British journalism as characterised by what he calls '**churnalism**', whereby journalists rely upon so-called 'facts' produced by spin doctors or public relations. He argues churnalism stems from cost-cutting, with journalists pressured to find stories quickly and at the lowest possible cost.

Marxism and news values

Marxists argue the news is manipulated by those who own and control broadcasting and newspapers. They view pluralist ideas on news values as naïve and argue they fail to understand the influence of both owners and advertisers. In addition, they question Davies' view that 'truth-telling' is the primary function of journalists. Marxists, like Neil Postman (1996), see the news as increasingly presented as '**infotainment**': little more than a diet of celebrity or sensational stories with little background story.

Neo-Marxism (Hegemonic) and news values

Neo-Marxists place more emphasis upon the (largely unconscious) biases of media personnel who are typically white, male and middle class. They are seen to take a 'reasonable', consensus-oriented view of the world, apparently impartial, but in fact ignoring inequality and exploitation in society.

Feminism and news values

What is considered newsworthy reflects a male outlook on life. Women's issues tend to be treated frivolously or simply ignored altogether. They point out how women's age and appearance often shape news stories. Women as victims are more likely to receive news coverage if they are white and pretty. Women's sport is rarely covered on television or newspapers.

Postmodernism and news values

Postmodernists emphasise how people are resistant to a single overall direction of media influence (as Marxists argue). Instead they argue that the news is 'read' in multiple ways. This reflects the increasing individualism of society alongside the diversity of meanings and identities that individuals possess in a highly fragmented society.

How do the media create moral panics?

An important aspect of news production is the way the media focuses upon deviant groups who form the basis of a **moral panic**. By defining such groups as problematic, the media can generate a public anxiety about the moral and ethical well-being of society. Some sociologists see moral panics as generated by leading and influential figures in society. These are called **moral entrepreneurs**, who react to sensational media reporting, thus stirring up more of a reaction.

Stan Cohen and mods and rockers

Stan Cohen (1972), in a classic but dated study, examined the conflict between mods and rockers in the 1960s. He showed how deviancy amplification led the media to grossly exaggerate their fighting, creating a 'moral panic' about these groups. He described how the media blew small-scale scuffles and vandalism out of all proportion by using headlines such as 'Day of Terror' and 'Town under siege'. Cohen identified three significant processes: 'symbolisation', 'exaggeration' and 'prediction' that form the basis of a moral panic. He noted that deviant groups are viewed as '**folk devils**' whose behaviour is associated with irresponsibility, lack of respect and moral degeneracy.

Hall *et al.* and mugging

They looked at the media portrayal of 'muggings' in the 1970s and how the media and the government used the moral panic it provoked as an excuse to strengthen policing methods. Hall argues that the moral panic served an ideological function at the time, with the media being used to whip up concern about 'the collapse of law and order', resulting in winning public support for new laws and tougher policing. Sociologists have drawn a parallel to a fear of terrorism being used to reduce civil liberties since 2001.

Sarah Thornton and rave parties

She studied the moral panic that erupted over 'rave parties' in the 1990s and found that the media panic about associated drug-taking simply added to the attraction for young people. She argues the 'Just Say No' campaign probably attracted more young people to the use of ecstasy as they realised adult society disapproved of their membership of the e-generation.

Volatility and short-termism of moral panics

Goode and Ben-Yehuda (1994) discuss the practice of most moral panics to begin suddenly only to disappear and be forgotten just as quickly. McRobbie and Thornton argue that moral panics are less frequent and harder to sustain these days.

Key Terms

Moral entrepreneurs = people like editors, religious leaders and politicians who see themselves as society's moral guardians by reacting to sensational media reports.

Moral panic = generally means a rapid and exaggerated media reaction to a deviant group that is viewed as threatening to moral fabric of society.

Folk devil = term associated with Stan Cohen to refer to deviant groups at the centre of 'moral panics'. Often their negativity is exaggerated by the media, and they are viewed generally as a threat to social order.

Grade boost

When answering questions on moral panics, ensure that your discussion covers more than just Cohen's discussion of mods and rockers. Use recent examples of moral panics and consider if the concept is as valid today compared to the past.

quickfire

④ Why do you think moral panics are a frequent feature of media news coverage?

Key figure

Frank Furedi (1994) makes a connection between moral panics and social change. He also links them to the wider concerns older people sometimes feel about society losing control as traditional norms and values appear less relevant.

Recent examples of moral panics: asylum seekers; youths wearing hoodies; knife carrying youth; paedophiles; binge drinking youth, ladette culture.

Key Terms

Copy-cat violence = when media violence is seen to trigger violence in real life.

Opinion leaders = influential and respected individuals who are looked up to by members of social networks.

Grade boost

Because all models (except the hypodermic syringe model) are active audience theories, this makes it difficult to generalise about the effects of the media. Although the media is undoubtedly a powerful institution, as witnessed by the success of advertising, the ability of audiences to interpret media messages remains and should not be underestimated.

quickfire

⑤ Why were the Frankfurt School so convinced the media had a powerful effect on society?

Key figure

Greg Philo (1999) is an important member of the GUMG who has made an important contribution to the cultural effects model and more recently to our understanding of how postmodernists, by challenging fixed reality, reject the media's ability to impose blanket effects on its audience.

To what extent does the media generate effects on its audience?

Media effects theories have existed as long as we have had a mass media. Sociologists are wary of simplistic correlations that the media shapes its audience, such as encouraging **copy-cat violence**. However, many theories claim that the media does influence behaviour in one way or another and the success of advertising supports this.

Hypodermic syringe model

This theory was developed in the 1930s and sees the media as having a powerful effect over a passive audience, which soaks up media messages like a sponge. It is associated with the Neo-Marxist Frankfurt School who witnessed the expert use and control of the media for propaganda purposes in Nazi Germany.

Active audience models

A variety of subsequent theories challenge the passivity of the audience. The first active audience theory was the 'two-step flow model' of Katz and Lazarsfeld (1965). They highlighted the role of '**opinion leaders**' in the community who interpreted and reinforced media messages to the rest of society. The 'uses and gratifications model' of Blumler and McQuail (1968) portrays the media rather like a supermarket shelf in which people pick and choose in order to use the media in a social way. David Morley (1980) developed these ideas further with his 'reception analysis model' in which he demonstrated how audiences adopt one of three interpretations of media messages: preferred, oppositional or negotiated. If people disagree with media messages they will challenge or adjust them.

Marxist cultural effects model

This sees the media as very powerful, containing strong ideological messages that are implanted in people's minds over time on a drip, drip, drip basis. This theory is supported by research from the Glasgow University Media Group (GUMG) which has examined how the media has shaped attitudes over time about strikes, the Gulf War and Israel. However, pluralists question the idea that the media reflects the interests of the capitalist élite and that we as an audience are little more than 'cultural dopes'.

Postmodernist theory

Postmodernists view society as fragmented and individualistic in nature. Consequently, they argue, it is impossible to make generalisations about media effects on the audience, since different people will have different reactions to the same media exposure. In many ways this is simply a development of Morley's 'reception analysis model'.

How are new technology and media impacting on the audience?

New technology refers to the digital hardware that has developed since the 1990s that offers an integrated access to communication and information. Examples include computers, **smart phones**, games consoles and multi-channel television. New media refers to this hardware technology but also the increasing convergence of digital material in one technology. So, for example, the smart phone makes and receives calls as well as email and access to the Internet.

Recent trends in new media

Raymond Boyle (2005) has highlighted the importance of convergence, which allows, for example, smart phones to offer facilities that used to be only available on separate platforms. Individuals can, for example, access and send photos, log on to their social network accounts and use applications to facilitate almost every aspect of their life, whether it is entertainment, sourcing information or finding directions through maps. Digital television and radio has led to a proliferation of channels. To Postmodernists this is evidence of extra choice. Marxists, however, argue that multiple channels provide very similar lightweight content and describe this as '**narrowcasting**'. Henry Jenkins (2006) regards the degree of interactivity as another key feature of new media. This has shifted choice and control to the user end of the media. We can choose who and what to interact with, such as with social networking and online gaming. It is also exemplified with Wikipedia whereby, in principle, every person can contribute a little of what they know to a pooling of knowledge.

The digital divide

It should come as no surprise that use of new media is particularly associated with young people, with talk of a 'generational divide', which has always been a feature of media use. Ofcom (2008) found that members of minority ethnic groups are also more likely to be active users of 'new media' than people generally. However, because media technology is expensive, the poor are the group most likely to be excluded from new media. They are less likely to have computers, Wi-Fi and broadband Internet access, smart phones and the latest gaming consoles. There also seems to be a greater confidence and usage of new media by men, although female usage is still significant.

Apple's iPhone and iPod are good examples of new technology that encourage a convergence of media.

Key Terms

Transnational corporations = large companies that trade globally but are usually based in the West, typically the USA.

Global village = romantic image of a global media of increasing interconnectedness associated with Marshall McLuhan.

Grade boost

Whilst Marxists see global media in terms of the cultural swamping of local values, the anthropologist Daniel Miller (1992) found that people make sense of US programmes through their framework of local practices and understanding.

quickfire

(7) What is meant by Coca-colonisation?

Key figure

Cohen and Kennedy (2000) support the argument of Miller above, arguing that in spite of a global media, people are not subject to cultural swamping but retain their local values and behaviours. However, they do accept there is a degree of absorption of global culture that gets mixed and matched with local culture.

How does globalisation impact upon the media?

The section on ownership highlighted the trend for media organisations to become increasingly global, **transnational corporations**. Global brands like CNN, Al-Jazeera, MTV and BBC are available via satellite and cable across the world.

Media via computers

The importance of computers in the expansion and use of the media cannot be over-stated. The Internet is an ever-increasing medium of global mass communication. Internet versions of most newspapers can be accessed along with most radio stations from around the world. With ever-greater download speeds from broadband, people are streaming films, downloading music, social networking, as well as playing computer games with friends and strangers across the world. In addition to providing entertainment, the Internet is a major source of information with governments, media companies and commercial corporations all embracing its potential to inform large numbers of people.

Global culture

Media advertising has helped create global products like Coca Cola, Disney and McDonalds, but the role of Hollywood films and television has equally helped the spread of Western cultural icons and values. Such is the dominance of the USA in global media that some commentators refer to this spread of cultural ideas as 'Americanisation' or 'Coca-colonisation'. Films like *Harry Potter*, television cartoons like *The Simpsons* and Swedish crime books like *The Girl with the Dragon Tattoo* trilogy are well known across the world. Yet as Roland Robertson (1992) notes, an interesting phenomenon of globalisation is how it can ironically spark a revitalisation in localisation. So in a world dominated by global media we also have Welsh (SC4) and Gaelic (BBC Alba) medium television channels in the UK.

Evaluation of a global media

As early as the 1960s the US media theorist Marshall McLuhan (1962) had a vision of the media generating a '**global village**' – apparent today with people communicating over vast distances through email, Skype, Facebook and Twitter. The expansion of media choice and diversity is applauded by Postmodernists. However, Marxists, such as Herbert Schiller (1991), see a global media as little more than the spread of US or Western culture (in the form of soap operas, sitcoms, a superficial obsession with celebrities and reality television) and the complete opposite of diversity.

How is gender represented in the media?

Traditionally the bulk of the mass media has been produced by men and targeted at men. Paul Townley (2000) argues there is still a significant **'glass ceiling'** that locates the female workers towards the bottom, although Pamela Creedon (1989) argues a 'gender switch' is occurring.

Traditional representations of gender

The media is accused of presenting gender roles and identity in narrow **stereotypical** ways. For example, until recently women were typically portrayed in domestic or traditional employment areas such as secretarial or caring roles. In addition, women were presented as invariably weak, vulnerable and in need of protection. Men, in contrast, were portrayed as breadwinners with characters who were strong and rarely showed emotions.

Postmodern representations of gender

Many Feminists argue that the representations above are still prevalent, with women's bodies blatantly used to sell products and provide sexual gratification such as the prevalence of pornography in tabloid newspapers and magazines like *Nuts* and *Zoo*. However, Frank Mort notes the sexualisation of the male body in advertisements, films and television, too. David Gauntlett (2008) argues that the postmodern media is so diverse that it is no longer possible to seriously discuss media gender representations, as they have become contradictory.

Media effects and gender

The use of seriously underweight models in the media has long been linked as a factor behind the growth of eating disorders. Whilst this cannot be conclusively proven, Becker *et al.* (2003) note that eating disorders only occurred in Fiji following the introduction of mainly US-based television. In the UK, the British Medical Association point to a growing dissatisfaction of men with their bodies and link this to media images of muscular men with tight 'six-pack' stomachs. The BMA conclude that gay men are particularly prone to body dissatisfaction and consequent eating disorders.

Representations of sexuality

Representation of sexuality in the media used to conform to a pattern of 'compulsory heterosexuality'. Homosexuality was a taboo subject, or if covered, gay people were typically presented as figures of ridicule or bad. Sociologists, like Rosalind Gill (2007), applaud the increased and varied portrayal of homosexual characters now in the media, but notes how they are portrayed in safe ways that avoid driving away audiences or advertisers.

To what extent do the media still portray women as sex objects? Are males increasingly portrayed as such?

Key Terms

Glass ceiling = barrier of male prejudice and discrimination that prevents women rising to top jobs.

Stereotype = a way of categorising people based on exaggerated, generalised and simplistic assumptions of a group's characteristics.

Grade boost

In gender representation questions, too many candidates focus on female coverage at the expense of a detailed analysis of how males are portrayed.

quickfire

⑧ Why does Gauntlett argue it is impossible to make generalisations about gender media messages anymore?

Key figure

Tuchman *et al.* (1978) introduce the emotive term 'symbolic annihilation' to refer to the way women's achievements are portrayed by the media as less significant compared to men. This applies to news stories, sports reporting and the predominance of men in the media.

Key Terms

New media = latest digital technology in the form of smart phones, Internet, satellite and cable television.

Islamophobia = prejudice against, hatred or fear of Islam or Muslims.

Grade boost

A useful contribution to any examination answer on ethnic minority representation is to recognise differentiation. For example, appreciate that the term 'Asian' covers a wide spectrum of groups with very different cultures, values, and religions. Within these groups there is also differentiation associated with age, gender and social class.

quickfire

⑨ In what ways are minority ethnic groups portrayed as a problem by the media?

Key figure

Elizabeth Poole (2002) studied the reporting of British Muslims in two broadsheet newspapers, *The Guardian* and *The Times*. She found that they were rarely treated as part of British society, but typically in stories that reinforced stereotypical assumptions about Muslim identities and activities.

How is ethnicity represented in the media?

Greg Dyke, when Director-General, stated in 2002 that the BBC was 'hideously white'. Many sociologists argue that a wide range of media still fails to reflect the multicultural society we live in. This is either by the underrepresentation of minority ethnic groups or through the reinforcement of stereotypes of such groups. For example, Toyin Agbetu (2006) sees black people as stereotyped into just three categories: criminality, sport and entertainment.

Portrayal of ethnic minorities as a problem

Minority ethnic groups form around 8 per cent of the UK population. Members of such groups argue that they are often underrepresented in the media, or when present, portrayed in narrow stereotypical roles or in terms of a problem. For example, the commonest coverage of ethnic minorities in the media is with regard to crime and violence. The recent media focus on gun and knife crime often made connections to ethnic minority communities and echoes the work of Hall *et al.* on how muggers were typically portrayed as black in the 1970s' moral panic. However, the media is less vocal on how minority ethnic groups are more likely to be victims of crime than the majority white population.

Portrayal of ethnic minorities as a threat

Many commentators see the media's coverage of minority ethnic groups over recent history as overtly racist in its portrayal of them as a threat to British values and way of life. Philo and Beattie (1999) suggest there have been a range of moral panics centred on issues such as immigration, economic migrants and asylum seekers. Since September 2001 there has been an orchestrated growth of **Islamophobia** with Muslims stereotyped as supporting terrorism, intolerant, misogynist (women haters) and different (Whitaker, 2002).

Is there scope for optimism?

In recent years there has been a greater visibility of minority ethnic groups as media personnel. In addition, there has been a growth in digital radio stations catering specifically for ethnic minorities as well as television channels produced outside the UK available on satellite and cable. The portrayal of minority ethnic groups within the UK and the developing world generally is still prone to negative coverage and more often than not seen as a problem.

How are class and age represented in the media?

Does the media reflect a class interest?

Marxists argue that the media reflects the class interests of its capitalist class owners. As the Frankfurt School noted, this is subtle, supporting capitalism by manipulating the audience as a **diversionary institution** offering escapism and entertainment. The media, through Hollywood, endless soaps and reality television, preoccupies the minds and interests of the proletariat. Neo-Marxist hegemonic theory sees the media as reflecting the views of white, male, middle-class journalists. Pluralists would argue that the media portrays a range of class interests and if it presents a certain world view, this is because it reflects consensus values. Postmodernists argue class has become meaningless, replaced by consumption as the main definer of identity. As a consequence the media reflects this by focusing on issues of style, fashion and consumption.

Representation of class

There is an overrepresentation of middle-class and professional people in the media, reflecting the background of most people who work within it. It is argued that the values and content of the bulk of **broadsheet newspapers** and **tabloids** like the *Daily Mail* and *Daily Express* represent middle-class values of decency, hard work and achievement. Working-class people are underrepresented and often portrayed in a negative way, such as being stupid or deviant as in *Shameless*. However, more media personnel now derive from working-class roots, such as Ant and Dec, and the portrayal of working-class life and struggles has been sympathetically portrayed in television drama and films like *Full Monty* (1997) and *This is England* (2006).

Representation of age

Many commentators see the media's coverage of age (childhood, adolescence, middle age and the elderly) as stereotypical. Images of childhood are invariably presented in a positive and romantic light. For example, issues of abuse and domestic violence are rarely covered other than in NSPCC advertisements. Adolescent youth are often portrayed as deviant or rebels of some kind. Recently, programmes like *The Inbetweeners* present a realistic account of the angst of male puberty along with common sexist male attitudes. The charity Age UK (2010) argues the media continues to promote ageist prejudices, either by rendering old people as invisible or presenting them as a problem.

Key Terms

Diversionary institution = Marxist term for any institution that takes the proletariat's mind off their exploited class position.

Broadsheet newspaper = titles like *The Times, Telegraph* and *Guardian*. Broadsheet refers to the size of page, although papers like *The Times* and *Guardian* now have tabloid-size pages.

Tabloid newspaper = titles like *The Sun, Mirror, Star*. Tabloid refers to page size.

Grade boost

Examiners like candidates who can make connections in their exam answers. Think about the interrelationship between age and gender within the media. Are younger attractive women still employed in contrast to older males of 'authority'? Think about news readers or weather presenters.

quickfire

(10) What is the social class background of most leading journalists?

Key figure

Curran and Seaton (2002) studied the content of The *Sun* and *Star* newspapers aimed at working-class audiences. They discovered an assumption that readers were not interested in political or economic stories but rather celebrity gossip and lifestyle. They question whether this becomes self-fulfilling.

Mass Media: Summary

We have identified the key points of this topic on the WJEC AS specification, i.e. the bare minimum you need to know. You may want to fill in further details to elaborate and personalise this content.

Ownership and control of media

- Concentration of ownership
- Globalisation and conglomeration
- Cybermedia
- Horizontal and vertical integration
- Synergy
- Technological convergence

News values

- Theory and news values: relative role of audience, owners, journalists/editors
- 'Window on the world' or manipulation by powerful media and ideology?
- Factors such as reference to elite person, elite nations, frequency, continuity, etc.
- Churnalism (Davies)
- Moral panics

New media and technology

- Digital revolution
- New media
- Digital divide

Theories of the media

- Pluralist theory
- Marxist (manipulative) approach
- Neo-Marxist (hegemonic) approach
- Postmodernist theory
- Feminist theory

Audience effects theories

- Hypodermic syringe model
- Two-step flow model
- Active audience models
- Uses and gratifications model
- Marxist cultural effects model

Media representations

- Gender, sexuality, ethnicity, social class, age, disability

Globalisation and the media

- Media via Internet
- Global culture

Exam Practice and Technique

Exam Advice and Guidance

How exam questions are set

WJEC AS Sociology aims to help students to:

- Acquire knowledge and understanding of contemporary sociological issues and debates.
- Acquire knowledge and understanding of sociological theories and use these as the framework for discussions about these issues.
- Acquire knowledge and understanding of sociological research methodology and the reasons behind research decisions.
- Acquire knowledge and understanding of the relationship between the research methodology used in research and the impact that this can have on the usefulness of the data collected.
- Make connections between topic areas and in so doing develop a clearer understanding of the complexities of the social world.
- Acquire the ability to demonstrate higher order skills of analysis and evaluation in sociological discussions using empirical evidence to argue a variety of theoretical standpoints.

Examination questions are written well in advance of the examination. They are written by the Principal examiner responsible for the unit. A committee of experienced examiners discuss the quality of every question and changes are made to the questions until the committee agree that they are appropriate. The questions are written to reflect the substantive content and the success criteria outlined in the specification.

How exam answers are marked

Exam answers are marked in relation to two assessment objectives:

- **Assessment objective 1 (AO1)**

  This is knowledge and understanding and it accounts for 55% of the marks at AS. You should be able to demonstrate knowledge and understanding of the specification and select accurate and appropriate knowledge to answer the questions. It is important not to learn by rote and instead you should aim to acquire an understanding of the social world. This should be demonstrated by answers that are clearly focussed on the question being asked. Answers should also demonstrate an appropriate use of sociological terminology, theory and, where required, empirical evidence. Detailed knowledge of sociological theories is not expected at this level. But a conceptual understanding of different perspectives is important for the construction of discussions in essays. The use of evidence to support a particular line of discussion is an important aspect of the success criteria.

- **Assessment objective 2 (AO2)**

  This is analysis and evaluation and accounts for 45% of the marks at AS. Analysis and evaluation are often referred to as higher order skills, as they are deemed to be more sophisticated than the AO1 skills. Analysis and understanding are often demonstrated at the same time and so if you are able to analyse effectively you are also demonstrating understanding. Analysis in simple terms is explanation and it includes the ability to make connections between lines of debate and/or evidence and the question being asked. Successful analysis involves interpretation of selected empirical evidence and explanation of what it shows in relation to theoretical debate and to the question.

  Evaluation involves the identification of the strengths and weaknesses of perspectives and evidence. It is a crucial component of well-written essays where questions ask candidates to assess or evaluate a particular view.

How exam questions are marked

Marks are awarded in skill domains or in other words specific skill areas. In Sociology these skills are split into:

- AO1 (assessment objective 1) which covers knowledge and understanding.
- AO2 (assessment objective 2) which covers analysis and evaluation.

It is crucially important to know what these skills are and how to demonstrate them in your answers.

AO1

- **Knowledge** When you write accurately about something that you know from your study of AS Sociology, and this knowledge is relevant to the question that you have been asked, you will achieve knowledge marks. You will also achieve knowledge marks if you use sociological terminology appropriately.

- **Understanding** Using knowledge that is relevant to the question being asked will show an understanding of the question. Connecting this knowledge to the question will show understanding, as will the use of examples or explanations.

AO2

- **Analysis** When you explain what something means or what a piece of evidence shows, you will achieve marks for analysis. When you link your explanation to the question you will also achieve marks for analysis. Analysis is a very important higher order skill that turns your answer from being a set of notes on a sociological topic or debate into a response to a question or command.

- **Evaluation** This is often regarded as the most demanding of the skills. When you point out the strengths or the weaknesses of a sociological perspective or piece of evidence, you will achieve marks for evaluation. You will not achieve marks for evaluation if you describe one view followed by a description of alternative views.

Analysis and evaluation often go hand in hand. It is possible to analyse without evaluating but it is not possible to evaluate without analysing if you want to achieve top band marks.

Try using this marking framework to help you to mark your own answers to SY1 1a questions.

Teacher mark	Student mark	**Knowledge & Understanding (AO1)**	
		3	**Knowledge** is detailed with the meaning of the term clearly defined with three accurate points **illustrated** with example(s).
		2	Some **knowledge** and understanding of the term. Two accurate points.
		1	Basic **knowledge** displayed with one accurate point but misunderstanding evider
		0	No relevant **knowledge** displayed.

Teacher mark	Student mark	**Analysis (AO2)**	
		2	Detailed **understanding is displayed through clear explanation.** Appropriate reference will be made to the item.
		1	Some **explanation** is offered.
		0	No **explanations** offered.

How is this applied to answers?

Q: *With reference to the item and your own knowledge explain the meaning of the term values.*

A: A value is a belief which the vast majority of society agrees upon. ① AO1 Values change over time as the culture of a society changes. ② AO1 A value could be seen as the reasoning behind a social norm. ③ AO1 For example, the majority of modern society chooses to wear a seatbelt, this is the norm, and the value behind it is the belief that human life should be protected. ④ AO2 Values can vary between ethnic groups and social classes. ⑤ AO1

This answer contains three accurate points and an example but no reference to the item so it gets 3 +1 = 4 marks.

Improving your exam performance

Understanding the command words

The command words in examinations provide the signposts for the skills that are being assessed. Understanding the meaning of these command words is the first step towards examination success.

Evaluate the view/assess the view/discuss: This command requires you to weigh up the strengths and weaknesses of a sociological view. It would inevitably involve a debate in which you would need to consider the value of the view in question and the value of alternative views. Note that you will never have an essay command asking you to describe a view, so if you do this in your response to a command asking you to evaluate, you should not expect to score high marks. Of course there would be a need to outline the view in order that you could then analyse and evaluate it but it is the analysis and evaluation of the view that will ensure high level success.

Outline/describe and explain: This command is easy to understand. You need to show your knowledge by outlining a view or concept and then explain (analyse) what it means. You might be expected to offer examples to clarify your explanation.

Useful phrases that can help you to respond appropriately to command words

It is very easy to write in a descriptive tone and, whilst this might not be so much of a problem in very short knowledge-based questions, it is a significant problem in essays.

Knowledge	Analysis/understanding/focus on the question	Evaluation
Fran Ansley says that …	This means …	The importance of this is …
Social control means …	If this is so then …	The value of this is …
Parsons believes …	From this we can see …	Nevertheless …
Allan and Crow suggest …	The relevance of this is …	The problem with this …
Functionalists say …	Hence …	Whereas …
Marxists claim …	Put simply …	A different view …
Weekes *et al.* suggest …	Therefore …	An alternative to this …
Charles Murray claims …	This suggests …	This does not take account of …
	This indicates …	Conversely …
		On the other hand …
		Similarly …

Planning answers

Top band essay answers need to have a logical structure. They need to be focussed on the debate and contain breadth of ideas (this means that you need a number of different points) and depth of analysis (this means that you need to explain your points and ensure that they are focussed on the debate).

This sort of plan could be adapted. For essays where you are asked to assess, evaluate or discuss a view you would need to add analysis and evaluation of the ideas that you have outlined.

Introductory paragraph:
What do we know?
What is relevant?
paragraph 1

Conclusion
paragraph 5

Reason 1 – A01
paragraph 2

How could this affect
divorce rates – A02
paragraph 2

Evidence to support
the reason offered
– A01 & A02
paragraph 4

**Reasons for
an increase
in divorce**

Reason 2 – A01
paragraph 3

Explain how this could
affect divorce rates – A02
paragraph 4

Explain how this could
affect divorce rates – A02
paragraph 3

Reason 3 – A01
paragraph 4

Evidence to support
the reason offered
– A01 & A02
paragraph 3

How to succeed in SY1

Approach the questions in this way:

1a) Write a definition of the term with some examples (drawn from the item and elsewhere) to show your knowledge and understanding.

1b) This is usually a socialisation/social control question. Write about sanctions, role models and so on. Sometimes you can talk about how behaviour is controlled by the various agents of socialisation and sometimes you could focus on gender socialisation as a working example of how people learn expectations of gender.

2a) This is a knowledge and understanding question that requires you to communicate what you know and explain it in relation to the question.

2b) This is always a discussion/debate so you must include argument here. Lots of evaluation all the way through your answer. Start with a plan of all of the points for and against.

Describe and explain each point and what it shows about the view in the question. For each point, explain and criticise it or support it. Using the phrases mentioned earlier can help you. For example:

- However (followed by a criticism)
- Nevertheless
- On the other hand
- Similarly (followed by a supporting point)
- In the same way …

So the essay answer must be a discussion which contains a spread of AO1 and AO2 skills.

Try this framework and try colour coding the skills.

Each section/paragraph of your essay should be more or less like this and in this way you will have all of the skills running through the whole essay.

[D]escribe a point or a view

[E] explain what it means

[S] upport the point or view with evidence

[I] nterpret what this shows

[R] efer to the question

[E] valuate, point out the strengths and weaknesses

Questions and Answers

This part of the guide looks at student answers to examination-style questions through the eyes of an examiner. There is a question on each topic in the AS specification with two sample answers – one of an A grade standard and one of a C grade standard. The examiner commentary is designed to show you how marks are gained and lost so that you understand what is required in your answers. At the end of each answer the commentary summarises the marks achieved and the reasons for gaining the grade.

The Compulsory Core

With reference to the item, explain the meaning of the term culture.

(5 marks)

The Welsh Flag

At any time in history it is possible to identify national and cultural identities. National identities are demonstrated by flags, costume, language and symbols which are important features of **culture**.

People translate their shared **culture** into norms of behaviour such as wearing their national dress or waving their national flag.

Culture is passed from one generation to the next, by families and by schools and other institutions.

Dress is a typical way of demonstrating shared culture and identity but language and other behaviours can also be used for this purpose.

Tom's answer:

Culture means a way of life. ① It might be a shared identity ② such as wearing national dress as the Item says. ③

Examiner commentary:

Summative comments

Tom's answer contains two knowledge points but the ideas are not explained, so the answer shows some but not detailed knowledge and understanding. For this reason Tom is awarded **2/3 for AO1** and **1/2 for AO2**. This would achieve a **C grade**.

Seren's answer:

The term culture refers to the combination of norms and values of any particular society. ① Values are the things that people think are important ② such as free speech ③, honesty or even nationality ④. When such things are important they are translated into norms or ways of behaving ⑤ such as showing that your nationality is important to you by waving ⑥ your national flag or wearing national dress as in the item.

Summative comments

Seren's answer contains six clear knowledge points and the final point demonstrates understanding. This answer was awarded **3/3 marks for AO1** and **2/2 marks for AO2** because it matches the top band mark descriptors. This would achieve an **A grade**.

Q & A

Describe and explain how any two agents of socialisation control behaviour.

(10 marks)

Tom's answer:

Two agents such as family and school can control behaviour. The family controls a child's behaviour by teaching them the norms and values of society from a young age, which allows them to grow up knowing this is how they should behave. If they behave in any other way, they are told that they are being deviant and possibly punished. Parents can use a variety of skills and techniques.

School is another agency that can control behaviour as children are taught discipline throughout their education. They know that if they misbehave, the outcome of their actions will be punishment which helps control behaviour as they don't want to be in trouble. Schools help to keep control of their behaviour as if they do well, they will get rewarded.

Seren's answer:

Behaviour is controlled through norms and values that people learn throughout the process of socialisation. They learn to respect others through primary socialisation where their parents reward and punish them using sanctions like being praised for good behaviour and grounded for bad behaviour. Parents use these sanctions to control their children's behaviour. Behaviour is also controlled in families through imitation of role models. Children copy the behaviour of their parents or other adults through games such as playing house.

Behaviour is also controlled in secondary socialisation in schools. Teachers impose formal social control through enforcing school rules. When school rules are broken, formal sanctions are used to punish children and discourage them from repeating the behaviour. For example, they might be given detention. They can also be praised for good behaviour through merit marks. Informal social control is also used in schools to control behaviour through disapproval or approval. Wearing school uniform is also a form of social control and behaviour can be controlled through formal and informal ways such as laws or just ignoring someone whose behaviour you don't like.

Examiner commentary:

Summative comments

Tom shows some understanding but his answer is not focussed on how behaviour is controlled. Tom talks about punishment and rewards but does not develop this with examples nor does he use key terms. For this reason Tom scores **3/5 for AO1** because he has made 'two accurate points'. Tom scores **3/5 for AO2** because he tries to explain both points but this explanation lacks detail. Tom scores a total of 6/10. This would achieve a **C grade**.

Examiner commentary:

Summative comments

Seren's answer demonstrates a sound understanding of how behaviour can be controlled. Key concepts are described in detail and examples are used effectively to show understanding. There are at least 'four points made' Seren does refer to two agents of socialisation and she refers to 'at least one sociological term in both agents described'. Because Seren's answer matches the top band descriptors she is awarded **5/5 for AO1** and **4/5 for AO2** giving her a total mark of 9/10. This would achieve an **A grade**.

Families and culture

Q & A

Outline and explain the variety of family types in contemporary society.

(15 marks)

Tom's answer:

① There are many different types of family in today's society, each with different family members, numbers and possibilities be they chances of divorce, new children, or new marriages. The first is the typical nuclear family consisting of a mother who cooks, cleans and looks after the children, And a father who provides invaluable resources for the family and is known as a breadwinner and typically two children, a girl and a boy. The family used to be the most common type of family though as of recent times it has been deteriorating.

② Another form of family is the lone parent family consisting of a single parent and children. This occurs through divorce or through the death of a partner. Another type of family is the step family which occurs when two parents divorce or a partner dies and the remaining partner dies and the remaining parent remarries bringing a stepmother or stepfather into the scenario.

③ Another, more secretive and less desirable family is the eggshell family when two parents or partners remain legally married for the sake of the children, financial reasons or others, but no real relationship between the partners exists.

④ Another form of family although it is not the conventional is cohabitation. When partners live together but are not married, this may be because of personal choice or for a more sexual relationship to ensue. Another family would be a homosexual family when two people of the same sex either marry or cohabit and may adopt children due to physical impossibilities.

Examiner commentary:

① Tom's answer begins quite well with the identification of a family type and some explanation of it. There is accurate knowledge and understanding evident in this opening paragraph.

② This paragraph begins with a word that has a descriptive and list-like tone and indeed the character of the paragraph is descriptive. Two more family types are identified but there is very little explanation. There are no examples and no reference to research.

③ This begins with the same list-like tone and there are some inaccuracies. There is a lack of analysis.

④ Again Tom starts his point with a word that gives a list-like tone to the answer. There is some assertion in this paragraph and only superficial analysis.

Summative comments

Tom's answer is characterised by description. This means that he may score marks for AO1 knowledge, but he is less likely to score marks for AO2 analysis. The answer scored **5/8 for AO1** because there were 'two or more family types described but the description lacked detail and was more superficial'. The answer scored **4/7 for AO2** because 'some attempt to explain the family types but this was brief and undeveloped'. This would achieve a **C grade**.

Seren's answer:

① Throughout history there have been many introductions to new kinds of families. According to functionalism the nuclear family is the cornerstone for all societies, this type of family includes two generations living under the same household, two parents with one or more children. A different version of the extended family would be the modified extended family where different family members live far apart but still contact one another through the use of telephone, email, frequent visits, etc.

② The patriarchal family is believed by feminists to be a male-dominated family, this is where the male brings in the income, makes the decisions and the woman is seen to serve the male, e.g. cooking and looking after the children. The matriarchal family is the complete opposite; this is where the female holds all of the power and runs the family. The symmetrical family type is where both husband and wife have equal roles; they both take part in house tasks as well as providing an income for the family.

③ Lone parent families are becoming increasingly popular; this is where only one parent is living in the house providing for one or more children. This type of family can be seen in mostly run down areas where many families are living in poverty and this might be a reason why parents divorce.

④ Reconstituted families or step families are ones which parents adopt a child or one where parents become remarried and the children live with another parent, these families are becoming more popular as the trends in divorce are increasing, allowing more parents to remarry.

⑤ Gay or lesbian families are also found in contemporary society. This is where a couple who are either gay or lesbian adopt a child to look after or they have a sperm donor which is the closest thing to having a child.

Examiner commentary:

① Seren presents some accurate knowledge points and two types of family have been identified with some explanations offered. So in this paragraph Seren demonstrates knowledge.

② Because the question refers to family types and not family structures the reference to patriarchal and matriarchal types is acceptable and demonstrates more knowledge and understanding of concepts. Seren's answer is beginning to develop in range and in depth/detail.

③ This paragraph identifies another family type, which adds to the breadth of Seren's answer, but adds some rather sweeping (assertive) statements. Nevertheless, there is an understanding of the link between lone parenthood and poverty.

④ Seren accurately identifies another family type, which further extends the breadth of the points made. However, the answer would benefit from some examples or references to research evidence to improve the sociological knowledge and the analysis.

⑤ Yet another family type is identified, meaning that Seren's answer has breadth of AO1. But it lacks any reference to evidence to illustrate the points made

Summative comments

Because Seren's answer 'identified three family types, which were described in detail but with no reference to research evidence' Seren's answer was awarded **6/8 for AO1**. It Scores **7/7 for AO2** because there is: 'detailed understanding shown through the explanation of most of the family types'. This would achieve an **A grade**.

Assess the view that the nuclear family can have a negative effect on its members.
(30 marks)

Tom's answer:

① There is a view that the nuclear family can have a negative effect on the family. To support this idea, sociologist Edholm believes that there is nothing normal or natural about the nuclear family and that it is a social construction. Feminists also support this view.

② There are two types of feminist. The radical feminists believe that the nuclear family is repressing the women. That the women do all the work and the men get all the credit. There is also the issue of domestic violence. Betsy Stanko claims that violence against women happens every 6 seconds and that it happens in families. Sociologists say that in the anthropology that the violence exists. Although it could be that the couple are not well suited or are both very strongly opinionated or they just know how to wind the other person up. It is said that men are more violent to women than female to men. Feminists say that this is because society is male dominated and the man needs to feel in control and powerful.

③ To oppose this view Jan Pahl found that there were four main types of control in families, wife control, husband control, wife control pooling and husband control pooling. It was found that the one with the pooling but the man in charge was the happiest.

④ Murdock studied 250 societies and found that there was a basic nuclear family in each one. The introduction of the new man helped argue against this view. Men are more accepting that a woman wants to work. Men are staying at home more and children are getting more support and love. It helps that there are two parents to socialise the child and bring it up correctly.

⑤ To conclude, I think that the view that the nuclear family can have a negative effect on its members is mostly wrong. There are more reasons and evidence to support the fact that it is positive. Although there are some compelling reasons why the nuclear family can be negative.

Examiner commentary:

① Tom begins by identifying a basic debate. Ideas are simplistic and undeveloped but this is an introduction and as such is an unsophisticated but effective opening paragraph.

② Tom gives a descriptive account of two types of feminism and he understands some feminist ideas about the family. He makes a very good reference to Stanko but does not link what she says to the debate. He then loses the focus of the debate and offers a descriptive account of reasons for domestic violence which is largely irrelevant to the question. Had Tom said that domestic violence and inequality in conjugal roles suggests that the nuclear family can have a negative effect on its members this paragraph would have been very much better.

③ Although Tom does make a reference to sociological research, the relevance of this is not clear. There is an implicit idea that families do not have a bad effect but this is not clearly stated. The example is not an effective one for the debate.

④ Though there is no reference to research evidence the points made in this paragraph are more relevant to the debate. However Tom does not use them well. He fails to explain how this could mean that the nuclear family does not have a negative effect on its members and so the relevance to the debate is implicit.

⑤ Tom makes an attempt to tie the ideas together and does make a reference to the focus of the discussion but what he says does not entirely reflect what was in his essay.

Summative comments

Tom's essay demonstrates some knowledge and understanding and for this his answer gets into band 3 for AO1. He understands the basic debate but does not make effective use of writers and for this reason Tom's answer scores **10/16 for AO1**. Tom's AO2 skills are weaker though there is 'some analysis or evaluation but there is juxtaposition of ideas rather than analysis or evaluation of them'. Tom's essay scores **8/14 for AO2**. So Tom's total mark is 18/30. This would achieve a **C grade**.

Seren's answer:

(1) The nuclear family was introduced by functionalist sociologists such as Murdock and Parsons. Murdock suggested that the family has four vital roles: economic stability, reproduction, sexual relations between parents and socialisation of children. This view has been heavily criticised by Marxists such as Engels who suggests functionalists have focused on the positive attributes of the family and ignored the negative role it may produce.

(2) Feminists such as Oakley view the family as patriarchal where the man is the head of the household and women are suppressed and inferior to the man's wants and needs. Marxist feminists go on to say that women are the 'takers of shit'. They absorb their husband's frustrations calming them down from the frustrations of capitalist society preventing revolution. Although a valid point, many sociologists disagree that this is the case.

(3) Marxists such as Karl Marx have a very negative view of the family, claiming that members are trapped within a family, women cannot live independently as they rely financially on their husbands, while working-class children are socialised into living in poverty.

(4) The nuclear family may have a negative effect on its members due to the 'dark side' of the family which was repressed in the early 60s due to the functionalist ideology of the family that see the family as a 'safe haven' from society. The dark side includes divorce that rips the family apart and causes distress to children along with domestic violence. In reconstituted families the majority of abusers are step parents leaving children trapped in a family of abuse.

(5) In Postmodern society Giddens suggested that women are still suffering from the nuclear family. The 'sandwich generation' resulting from an aging population means women are stuck caring for young children and elderly relatives. Although men still have to provide the main economic earnings for the family, the recession and other economic factors mean that women are forced into taking part-time work to support the family. This led to a 'triple shift' for women firstly taking care of the children, which is still done primarily by the woman, then taking on part-time work, before returning home to do the domestic chores. Although conjugal roles are changing, women still do the majority of the house work according to Oakley.

(6) What about children? In modern society, as the amount of dual earner families rises to 60% and parents become financially rich but time poor, giving in to consumer demands for electrical goods, children are forced to play with an 'electronic babysitter'. This in turn has led to poor socialisation which according to Marxists is the reason for such high crime rates.

(7) In conclusion although the nuclear family appears to have irreplaceable functions, the nuclear family can have many negative effects on its members such as repression of women, poor socialisation of children and the general term for the dark side of the family.

Examiner commentary:

(1) Seren identifies the basic debate. She makes some errors but the introduction is effective.

(2) Seren begins to construct the debate in this section of her essay and uses research evidence and theory to do so. She also attempts an explicit if not sophisticated evaluation of the points made. Had Seren added some evidence to support the criticism, this would have been an excellent paragraph.

(3) Another section that demonstrates accurate knowledge and understanding but a link to the debate would have improved it.

(4) Though there are some sweeping (assertive) statements Seren clearly understands the debate and uses sociological terminology effectively.

(5) This is a very good section full of accurate knowledge and understanding. There is breadth and depth in this paragraph. Seren could have linked the points made to the debate to improve her AO2 skills.

(6) This section demonstrates more accurate knowledge and uses terminology to demonstrate understanding. A good paragraph, even though the link between poor socialisation of children, high crime rates and Marxism is inaccurate.

(7) The concluding paragraph is focussed on the central debate and effectively identifies the main points.

Summative comments

This essay demonstrates 'detailed knowledge and understanding of critical views of the family', 'most ideas are developed so that the answer has depth and breadth and there is reference to writers and theory' though more of this would have given Seren full marks. Seren's answer matches the descriptors for band 4 **AO1** and **scores 15/16**. For AO2 Seren's essay demonstrates 'detailed understanding with an evaluative tone'. The essay is focussed on the debate. There could have been more explicit evaluation and analysis. Seren scores **13/14 for AO2** giving her essay a total of 28/30. This would achieve an **A grade**.

Youth Culture

> Outline and explain reasons why many youth cultures are often seen as masculine.
> *(15 marks)*

Tom's answer:

Examiner commentary:

① Many youth cultures are often seen as masculine and they ignore girls. Boys are more likely to have subcultures of their own and hang out on streets.

① Tom has not used the opening paragraph to set the scene for the debate. However, he has offered a reason which he should have gone on to explain.

② Many boys are involved in subcultures such as skinheads. Hebdige put forward the idea that they were a working-class youth culture. They wore traditional working-class manual worker clothing. Girls were often ignored. However, girls did have a culture of their own known as bedroom culture which McRobbie and Garber talked about. This is where girls hang out in bedrooms talking about boys, sex, doing each other's make up, whereas boys would hang out on the streets with other boys. For example, Mod boys would ride around on their scooters.

② This paragraph is better. There is reference to studies and some detailed knowledge of youth cultures and how they behaved. However, Tom does not use his knowledge well. There was an opportunity for him to explain that because boys were out and visible and girls were in their bedrooms this could be why youth cultures are often seen as masculine.

③ Many boys were more likely to have committed crime because men are more lenient to girls and would let them off and not see girls as a typical offender. However, girls are becoming more involved in youth culture and they are now not seen as so masculine because before, many youth cultures were male based but girls are becoming more like them because of girl power. They have more self-confidence and are becoming more like men. Katz said that girls are becoming more like a ladette and behaving like men whereas boys are unsure about their masculinity in society and some are becoming more macho against girls like in Hip-Hop.

③ This paragraph starts badly because it makes an assertion about girls and crime. However the point about youth crime appearing to be masculine is relevant to the debate and linked to the previous point about girls being more home based. Again this could have been linked effectively to the question but it was an AO2 opportunity lost.

④ Boys are more likely to hang out on the street. However, there is now a dance culture and Chatterton says girls can join. Kearney talks about club culture where everyone is welcome but that girls are allowed to join because parents are stricter on girls. Some boys were involved in youth cultures because parents allowed boys more freedom but saw boys as assertive and able to look after themselves.

④ This paragraph remains focussed on the behaviour of males and females but it could have been developed to emphasise that as the behaviour of girls changes and they have more freedom they are becoming more explicitly associated with youth cultures. Tom's answer is really about the invisibility of girls resulting from parental control. The final sentence is focussed on the question but the link is implicit.

Summative comments

Tom's answer gained 10 marks overall, **AO1 was worth 6/8** because there were two or more reasons with supporting evidence. The answer was awarded **4/7 for AO2** because the explanations lacked detail and were undeveloped. Tom had the potential to gain an excellent grade. He refers to a range of writers and evidence and makes some very good points. However, he did not make it clear why the points were relevant to the question. This would achieve a **C grade**.

Seren's answer:

① Many youth cultures are often seen as masculine because most of the research has been centred on males. This is known as malestream. In the pre-1980s, a lot of research was conducted into spectacular youth cultures. Marxists did most of the research into such cultures and being male, they totally ignored the girls.

② A good example of a youth culture being seen as male is the skinheads. Cohen carried out research and his findings portrayed this as a group consisting of white working-class males. They were portrayed as violent and aggressive, taking part in violent racist attacks known as 'aggro'. They were described as showing working-class masculinity and this means they were portrayed as a masculine group. Some youth cultures are known to treat girls with disrespect, so in Hip-hop, girls are called 'Ho's' and other nasty things.

③ Another reason why many youth cultures are seen as masculine is that a study by McRobbie and Garber acknowledges the focus on males in youth cultures and made findings about girls in youth cultures. From their research, they concluded that girls did have a part to play in youth cultures, although they were often overlooked because they were less obviously deviant and less interesting to male sociologists. They suggested that due to the socialisation of girls and the supervision that they undergo in adolescence, they adopt a more hidden bedroom culture. This is normally in pairs, when girls discuss boys, sex and make-up tips. The privacy of this youth culture is why it is overlooked and males are seen to be dominant in youth culture.

④ Another reason why many youth cultures may be seen to be male is the media. Thompson suggests that the media focussed on spectacular youth cultures and caused moral panics with violence. The media portray youth cultures as masculine and violent because it made interesting reading. If youth cultures are seen as masculine, then more boys will be attracted to them than girls.

Examiner commentary:

① This is a very good opening paragraph that not only makes it clear that the candidate understands the debate but also uses a key term appropriately, demonstrating knowledge and understanding. A good start.

② Seren demonstrates AO1 skills by referring to a named writer and then links this to the debate, suggesting that this was why the youth culture was masculine. Seren offers some explanation of the low profile of girls and brings this into a more contemporary setting with her reference to Hip-hop.

③ Seren clearly identifies two reasons in this paragraph and she connects the two in her explanations. She suggests that youth cultures are malestream because the way girls are socialised keeps them out of the public eye. She also suggests that this made girls less interesting to sociologists and so this is another reason why youth cultures are often seen as masculine.

④ Another clearly identified reason is offered in this paragraph which means that the answer has breadth. The reason is then explained giving the answer depth. Seren even suggests that youth cultures might actually be masculine because the way that they are portrayed attracts males.

Summative comments

This answer contained 'detailed knowledge and understanding'. It contained 'three or more reasons and there were at least two references to research evidence'. For this reason the answer was awarded **8/8 for AO1**. There was 'detailed understanding shown through the explanation of the reasons'. The answer was focussed on the question. For this reason the answer was awarded **7/7 for AO2** in other words it scored full marks. This answer met all of the requirements of the mark scheme. It matched the mark band descriptors and so it scored the marks. This would achieve an **A grade**.

Assess the view that spectacular youth cultures are a thing of the past.

(30 marks)

Tom's answer:

① Spectacular youth cultures seem to be a thing of the past. Cohen said that youth culture was meaningful and people would defy capitalism by their appearance. Post modernist would argue that youth cultures are a thing of the past and that neo-tribes are the present. Neo tribes are youth culture with a pick and choose of various styles.

② Spectacular youth cultures were class based and being deviant. Neo tribes are seen as not being class based as they have a large number of ethnicities. Redhead studied the subculture called rave and there are no ethnic boundaries. Spectacular youth cultures were long lived and still present today as people still listen to the same music such as rockers, skinheads, punks. Neo tribes are short lived because of the fluid and fragmented nature. Spectacular youth cultures are known for their characteristics, their norms and values. Now, Neo tribes are blurred and unclear of their opinions.

③ However, there are exceptions. There have been recent youth cultures that have meaning such as even though the British Nationalists are focused upon racism and not liked, they still have meaning.

④ There are exceptions to long lived youth cultures such as Hippies and punks. There are still some spectacular youth cultures also in the modern era, There are Goths, moshers, chavs. There are arguments that punks were not class based because upper class art students would join the youth culture. There are still class based youth cultures to the present day and frowned upon by the upper class such as chavs in Burberry. They are associated with poverty and crime.

⑤ There are less spectacular youth cultures but there seem to be less around. In this era, it is thought that capitalists formed a pick and mix society as a way to stop people from defying society and youth cultures have to take their meaning from the back catalogue.

Examiner commentary:

① In an opening paragraph, it is best to explain the nature of the debate. This question is really asking if there has been a change in the nature of youth culture. It is more specific than that Tom understands this point; it is clear from the structure of the argument that he is able to examine two different points of view. But Tom fails to clarify his understanding or the point he is trying to make.

② In this paragraph, Tom makes a number of points to support the view that spectacular youth cultures are a thing of the past. He can be credited for this even though it is not clear that he knows what spectacular youth cultures actually are. His understanding is implicit, rather than clearly stated.

③ Now Tom is exploring an opposite point of view and he could have added detail by developing this point.

④ This material could have been developed more carefully. Tom understands that there are class-based youth cultures, and that they are spectacular. He could have improved his AO2 by linking the points to the debate.

⑤ In this paragraph there are some potentially relevant ideas that could have been developed and linked to the debate.

Summative comments

Tom's answer gained 18 marks in total. **AO1 was worth 9/16** because the answer demonstrated 'some knowledge but this was undeveloped'. **AO2 was awarded 9/14** because there was 'some sociological understanding, some evaluative points and a debate'. Tom understood the debate, but missed important detail and failed to develop his points or link them to the debate. There is a superficial quality to the answer, so it is worth a total of 18/30. This would achieve a **C grade**.

Seren's answer:

① Postmodernists say that youth cultures are a thing of the past. They say that youth cultures have now turned into Neotribes. These Neotribes are blurred, not class based. They are meaningless and short lived. This is opposite to the spectacular youth cultures of the 1970s and the pre-1980s.

② Postmodernists such as Bennett on his research into urban dance culture say that class is no longer a factor in youth movements. His research suggests that in urban dance culture, a wide variety of people from different backgrounds mix. He also says that there is no one distinctive style. From the interviews he conducted and the observations he made, he concluded that the style in music and clothes displayed was eclectic. However, Marxists would argue that class is still a factor as working-class people may not be able to go out clubbing like middle-class people could.

③ Another reason why some sociologists might say youth cultures are a thing of the past is to do with the media-saturated society we live in. Millions of images are continuously thrown at youth and this gives them many more options to choose their own style. Sociologists such as Ted Polemus say we live in a supermarket of style where we have many options to be able to adapt and choose style. Our society is also a 'pick and choose' society, so sociologists such as Willis suggest that youth consumption isn't a passive one, but a creative one. However, Willis is criticised for underestimating the effect capitalism has on the consumption patterns of young people.

④ Another suggestion why some people may think spectacular youth cultures are a thing of the past is because of how the youth cultures that form in postmodern society are meaningless compared to the Marxists views of youth cultures in the pre-1980s which were based on meaning. Then, those cultures were said to be about the rebellion of youth against capitalism. Hebdige says that now youth cultures are not so spectacular, this is because of a process known as incorporation. This is when even the most subversive cultural products are used in advertising and they become familiar. Meaning is consequently stripped from them. An example of this was the punk band, the Clash, which was used for advertising jeans. However, some would argue that it does not take away from meaning, it just draws attention to it and people add a new layer of meaning.

⑤ The view that spectacular youth cultures are gone may depend on how you would define them. If you define them as a sort of style, meaning and purpose then they do exist in our society. A good example of this is the Goths. However, the media sensationalised spectacular youth cultures of the pre 1980s were involved then in politics, but some people then may just have liked the styles and the fashion rather than having the meaning. Eventually the fashions of the youth cultures were just incorporated into mainstream society and were just styles.

Examiner commentary:

① This is a clear and accurate opening paragraph in which Seren demonstrates knowledge and understanding. She also makes a connection between the view and a theoretical perspective and this is an excellent way to begin the essay.

② Seren uses theory and evidence for and against the view. This is countered with the Marxist view. To make this paragraph even better Seren could have made a more explicit link to the debate stating what this evidence suggests about spectacular youth cultures being a thing of the past. Nevertheless an impressive paragraph.

③ This paragraph explores more accurate points and utilises evidence and key terminology very effectively. The notion that choice is only choice for some could have been further developed but even so this is another good paragraph full of knowledge and understanding of the debate.

④ Seren does not explain in detail exactly what she is trying to say in this paragraph. Despite this, the potential for a high-level, sophisticated line of debate underlies the points made. Had they been clearly explained and linked to the debate, this could have been an excellent section.

⑤ This paragraph tries to sum up the discussion and come to a conclusion about spectacular youth cultures. The point about definitions is a good one and the critical, speculative tone of the conclusion is an effective end to the essay even though it could have been more explicit.

Summative comments

Seren demonstrates detailed knowledge and understanding and she has referred to evidence and research. Her answer contains 'detailed and wide ranging ideas supported by examples and evidence'. For this reason, Seren scored **14/16 for AO1**. The answer demonstrated 'detailed understanding shown through the examples and evidence cited. There is an evaluative tone and an assessment of the view'. For this reason, the essay scored **13/14 for AO2** giving Seren a total of 27 marks out of 30. With clearer analysis and more explicit evaluation Seren could have scored even higher marks. This would achieve an **A grade**.

Research Methods

Using material from the item and elsewhere, explain the meaning of the term survey. *(10 marks)*

A research project was conducted into cultural life in Britain. A survey of the UK population looked at how age, class and gender affected taste in mass media and leisure interests.

The survey used a random sample of nearly 1600 people. An additional quota sample of 230 members of British ethnic minority communities was included to make sure that this group was fully represented. This was followed up by household surveys of 44 homes.

Statistical information was gathered on the sample and it was discovered that only 12% of the population attended opera, with a similar percentage attending bingo. Ethnic minorities are less interested in soap operas than the general population.

Adapted from the ESRC website

Tom's answer:

The meaning of a survey is the breaking down of a topic into questions. A survey is a quantitative and qualitative method. There are different types of surveys such as structured interviews which is a face to face conversation between an interviewer who asks the questions and an interviewee who answers the questions. Another survey is postal surveys/ questionnaire where a topic has been broken down into questions and is either posted out or given out. Another survey is a longitudinal survey where a survey is taken over a long period of time, e.g. 10 years old, 20 years old, 30 years old, etc. This type of survey is normally taken every ten years. These questions are normally asking about a person, e.g. how many people live with you? A survey is questioning a group of members from the population. Surveys generally look at groups such as age, class, gender, etc. This can be seen in a survey of the UK population. A survey is to find out answers and details about the population and its members.

Examiner commentary:

Summative comments

Tom has produced a reasonable answer here but it is rather short. In addition, there is no direct reference to the item other than obliquely towards the end. Note that it is not possible to get into the top mark band without a clear reference to the item. However, there is generally good understanding as to what a social survey is, which is where the bulk of his marks derive from. Whilst surveys can collect quantitative and qualitative data, they are particularly associated with a quantitative approach and this point should have been made. It is a pity there are not clearer examples used, particularly referring to actual sociological social surveys. Tom's answer gained **4/6 AO1 marks** and **2/4 AO2 marks** giving 6/10 marks overall. This would achieve a **C grade**.

Seren's answer:

① The term survey means a set of questions similar to a questionnaire such as that referred to in the item where the researchers wanted to investigate cultural attitudes by asking questions. Other examples of surveys include the Census and Sewell's study of black schoolboys. Social surveys normally take the form of questionnaires but can also take place using structured interviews.

② There are many different types of surveys such as longitudinal surveys such as the 7-Up programme. This is when the researcher visits a person and they complete the survey, they then revisit the person every 5, 10, 15 years or whatever. This gains data that might have changed as the person grew up. Another type of survey is postal surveys. These are mailed to the respondent who completes the survey and then sends it back. The advantages of using surveys are that they are cheap and easy to administer. Questions are drawn up, printed, copied and sent away. It does not involve hard work, e.g. postal surveys; the researcher just has to wait for the respondent to send the survey back. Many surveys produce quantitative data, statistical and numerical data that is easier to collate, making it easier for the data to be analysed, quantified and compared.

③ The disadvantages of surveys are that only certain questions can be asked. People will not answer emotive questions such as asking a woman how old she is. Questions that are difficult will also not be answered, such as what is your view on transvestites, and ambiguous questions which have two meanings such as are you gay?

④ Also the disadvantages of postal surveys, such as Sheer Hite's magazine questionnaire study of women's sexual experiences, is that people may not respond and the negativities of longitudinal surveys are that the respondent may have passed away or moved house or chose to stop continuing with the survey.

⑤ In my opinion, surveys are a good way to gain data on research. It is an easy way to ask people certain things and it is quick and cheap to carry out.

Examiner commentary:

① Seren demonstrates good understanding as to what social surveys are in this first paragraph. There is an explicit reference to the item. She includes reference to Sewell and the Census needed to get into the top mark band. However, she makes an assumption that the survey in the item used questionnaires, this is not actually stated.

② This is quite a long and detailed paragraph. The sample of 7-up, whilst being a longitudinal study, is not strictly sociological and is an example of an observational study. There is a good discussion of different types of social surveys followed by a recognition that social surveys tend to collect quantitative data. This is evaluated in terms of its ease of analysis.

③ Seren deserves credit for evaluating social surveys in terms of disadvantages, but this paragraph is of variable quality. She identifies some problems but would be better to focus on practical problems associated with social surveys.

④ The theme of disadvantages is continued here, looking specifically at problems with postal surveys. Seren identifies several important points in this paragraph..

⑤ Seren should not personalise her answer using comments like 'in my opinion'. She should be careful making sweeping statements that surveys are 'quick and cheap'. Whether a social survey is a quick and cheap means of carrying out research really depends upon the nature of research and the size of the group being surveyed.

Summative comments

Seren has produced a thoughtful answer here but it is not perfect. She demonstrates good knowledge and understanding of social surveys and gives several examples for which she is rewarded. She also recognises the connection to quantitative data and evaluates this in terms of ease of analysis, but fails to discuss the implications of what limited qualitative data means. To have improved this answer she could have made more reference and use of the item. Seren would have improved this answer with more explicit reference to studies using surveys; this would support her analysis. Seren's answer gained **5/6 AO1 marks**, **3/4 AO2 marks**, making 8/10 marks overall. This would achieve an **A grade.**

Q & A

With reference to the item (see previous question) and sociological studies, explain why different forms of sampling are used in social research. *(20 marks)*

Tom's answer:

① When a researcher conducts a research, especially when using questionnaires/surveys, the choice of sampling is significant for the result. There are many different forms of sampling techniques, some of them are as they are mentioned in the item; random sample, quota sample and then there are also stratified sample and opportunity sample.

② Random sample is when the sample is chosen randomly from a target population, picking every fifth, tenth or twentieth person. This was used by Rosenthal and Jacobson in their Pygmalion classroom study and is the most unbiased sample technique and it provides the researcher with a representative sample which enables the result to be generalised to the rest of the population. However, it could be argued that it is not completely random as the number chosen (fifth, tenth or twentieth person, etc.) may be biased. Still, it is one of the most used samples techniques, because of its strong advantages.

③ Another sample that is often used is stratified sample. Here, depending on the aim of the research, the sample is divided into different classes or categories. For example, they might be categorised in groups of age, race, or gender. This is a sample often used when comparing trends or opinions between groups or categories. However, whilst this sample is generally representative, it may not be.

④ Sometimes opportunity samples are used. This is an advantage if lack of time is an issue. Laud Humphreys could be seen to have used an opportunistic sample in his observational study of homosexual tearooms. However, this sample is also lacking representativeness and cannot be generalised to the whole population as the sample might be dominated by one type of characteristic, i.e. many females, old people or people very interested in the research topic.

⑤ As shown in the item, researchers choose different forms of sampling depending on the aim of the research. If the aim is focused on the cultural differences, like in the item, the researcher is more likely to choose stratified sampling rather than opportunity sampling. Also if the researcher does not have much funding, he or she is more likely to choose the cheapest and easiest sampling technique.

⑥ This is why different forms of sampling are used; they are chosen due to the relevance to the topic of a researcher's investigation, which enables them to achieve the most desirable result.

Examiner commentary:

① Tom begins this answer well with an immediate attempt to address the question in the first sentence, although 'significant for the result' is vague and needs elaborating. A range of sample types is listed and reference is made to the item.

② Systematic sample is erroneously described here as random sampling. The issue of representativeness is important in evaluating sampling but the connection of this here to the size of sample is not made. The assumed advantages in the last line should be identified clearly.

③ Good start to this paragraph, Tom defines stratified sample quite well. However, its justification for use is poor and the last sentence is wrong. It is often used precisely to ensure that it is representative compared to other sample types.

④ This is a generally good paragraph that attempts to explain why opportunity samples might be used. However, other reasons for its use could have been explored. Paragraph ends well with good evaluation of how it might lack representativeness.

⑤ Whilst Tom could have looked at why researchers use other sample types such as snowball samples, this paragraph is focused upon the question.

⑥ There is an attempt by Tom to respond back to the question in this conclusion but it is a little vague as to why.

Summative comments

Tom has produced quite a good answer that addresses the question but doesn't really unpack why different sample types are used or provide examples from sociological research. His introduction and conclusion both refer directly to the question but the main body of his answer needed to explore, with examples, the reasons behind using different samples more explicitly. Tom's answer gained **8/12 AO1 mark**s, **5/8 AO2** marks making 13/20 marks overall. This would achieve a **C grade**.

Seren's answer:

① Researchers use samples since it is rarely possible to study every person in the target population they are studying. However, providing their sample is representative then they should still gain the same results from their research as if they had surveyed or interviewed everyone in the target population. Sample types include random, systematic, voluntary, snowball and stratified.

② The commonest type of sample used is probably the random sample. This is effectively like putting the names of all those being researched into a hat. Therefore everyone in the target population has an equal chance of being chosen. O'Beirne used this sample type in her study of religion by contacting households chosen at random. Researchers use this method as it is simple and straightforward. However, there is a danger that if the sample is too small, it will not be representative.

③ A stratified random sample is made up of the groups in the same proportion as they occur in the population being studied. So if ethnic minority groups made up 10 per cent of the population then the researcher would ensure they were 10 per cent of the sample. Helen Haste ensured her sample had characteristics of gender, age, ethnicity, class in her studying of young people and mobile phones. A strength of this sample is that it ensures that a sample is representative, meaning to ensure that it has the characteristics of the target population.

④ Sometimes researchers have difficulty gaining access to the population they want to study. In such cases they use different samples to the two discussed so far. They may rely upon people volunteering themselves, such as advertising for respondents. For example, they may wish to study people who have experienced domestic violence. Sheer Hite used a voluntary sample when she included her questionnaire on women's sexual experiences in women's magazines and asked women to post them back to her. The problem with any voluntary or opportunistic sample is that the people who come forward to participate may not be typical of the wider population.

⑤ Another type of sample used for elusive and difficult to find groups is the snowball sample. This is when one person is found who is willing to take part, such as James' study of gypsies and travellers. James gained all her sample through 'gatekeepers' who put her in contact with others, who, in turn, introduced more respondents. This type of sample is often used when researching deviant or criminal groups such as drug takers or groups like paedophiles who keep a low profile in the community. The problem with snowball samples is that they may not be representative if they are too small or the people found are not typical.

⑥ So it is clear that researchers use different samples according to the circumstances of their research and the populations they are studying. They are often obliged to use a certain type in order to be effective in their research and access the people they are studying.

Examiner commentary:

① Seren begins her answer with a good first paragraph. She explains the use of samples in relation to the size of the target population. There is good knowledge of sample types displayed here.

② Another good paragraph that defines and explains why random samples are commonly used. She enhances her answer by including the research of O'Beirne as an example of this type of sample. Good AO2 evaluative point about this sample lacking representativeness if too small.

③ Stratified random samples are explained and justified here by Seren, although the fact that each person in each group has a random chance of being chosen for each category is not explained. She brings in a good example of Haste's study of mobile phone. It gains good AO2 marks at the end for justifying its use.

④ The reasons why researchers use a voluntary sample are explained. Seren offers a good illustration and includes the research of Hite as a real-life example. Good evaluation of the problems of using this type of sample gains AO2 marks.

⑤ Snowball samples are explained by Seren here and their use justified. The applied example of James's study of gypsies and travellers is given and the use of this sample evaluated gaining AO2 marks.

⑥ The strength of this final paragraph is that there is an attempt to focus explicitly back to the question.

Summative comments

Seren has produced a detailed and excellent answer that has good focus to the question and makes an explicit attempt to explain why different sample types are used. As an answer it employs technical language and attempts to explain why samples are used. In terms of the mark scheme she makes reference to several sociological research studies. She could have discussed systematic sampling. Seren's answer gained **12/12 AO1 marks**, **8/8 AO2 marks** making 20/20 marks overall. This would achieve an **A grade**.

Education

Q&A

Outline and explain labelling theory in education. *(20 marks)*

Tom's answer:

① Labelling theory states that children are defined and labelled by teachers, other pupils and parents. This can lead to self-fulfilling prophecy. A teacher makes an assumption about a pupil and labels him a 'dupper' or 'bright'. The child then starts to behave like the label and will stop trying in a subject and this means that there will be underachievement and failure. The teacher has a preconceived opinion of the pupil and the child will stop trying to succeed. The teacher will develop a view of the child that is difficult to shift and then the pupil will live up to that label.

② Labels can be produced by the ways that schools work. Children may be placed in lower sets and then they are labelled and start acting like the label. If the child excels in some subjects, they will be labelled as bright and then other pupils and the teachers will respond to the label.

③ Labelling can lead to the underachievement of many pupils. Due to a bad label, they will start to believe the label and this will lead to a self-fulfilling prophecy. Some will go on to develop an anti-school subculture and they will act up to their label. Some want to be seen as 'macho' in school. They are then seen as unruly or disrespectful and then the teachers will not support them and they will fail in school.

④ Labelling has a huge effect on a child's progress in school. They will continue to believe that they are not good enough and are then channelled in to low paid work. In my opinion, the labelling theory is very negative and can change someone's life. Teachers should remain unbiased and ignore where a pupil is from, or their background and they should behave the same to all pupils.

Examiner commentary:

① Note the way that Tom has made an excellent clear statement of what labelling theory says and how it works. However, rather than develop the point with new knowledge or some evidence, Tom goes on to say the same thing in a number of different ways. This happens throughout the answer.

② This shows understanding of institutional elements to labelling, but rather than developing this good point with evidence or elaboration, Tom returns to explaining labelling theory in very much the same terms as before!

③ There is excellent use of technical language. This is evident throughout the paragraph. Ethnographic evidence could be used to support the point, for example Jackson's study of lad culture would be useful.

④ It is not good style to bring yourself into an essay. Sociology should be value-free and objective, so an opinion is not as useful as a piece of evidence. Labelling theory is just that, a theory. Tom has forgotten that it should be evaluated with evidence and has criticised teachers instead. He is not explaining the theory, but accepting that labelling takes place in an uncritical fashion. A better ending would be to suggest that there is evidence that pupils can reject labels and achieve despite negative stereotyping.

Summative comments

Tom's answer gained 13 marks overall, **AO1 was worth 7/12** and **AO2 was awarded 6/8**. Tom had the potential to gain an excellent grade as labelling theory is clearly explained and the language of sociology is fully applied to the answer. It lacks the specific reference to supporting evidence or to studies that have investigated labelling theory. There is little reference to which pupils attract negative labels or why labelling of such pupils may occur. Tom has met many of the assessment objectives for this element of the course. His answer is weaker because it lacks the specific detail and is less fully developed than Seren's answer. This would achieve a **C grade**.

Seren's answer:

① Labelling theory is where teachers, and the education system, stereotype a group of people to be something before they really know them. Teachers apply labels such as 'trouble maker' and 'waste of time' to those whom they believe are not going to be worthy of an education. This is usually aimed at working-class or African-Caribbean boys who show very different attitudes to Asian girls who are stereotyped to be very interested in education and success.

② Labelling can seriously downgrade a child's progress as the teachers have already got an opinion on the child before they have been given a chance to prove themselves. Teachers may make a prophecy that the African-Caribbean child will underachieve; therefore they do not spend time on those boys. This will result in those boys feeling like there is no point as they are predicted to fail anyway. Sewell found that many such boys reacted by rejecting school and the teachers and behaving in a negative fashion to racism in schools. Thus it would seem to teachers that they have predicted correctly, therefore resulting in African-Caribbean boys underachieving and thus reinforcing the stereotype.

③ Also, if teachers are stereotyping African-Caribbean boys, this could be evidence that they are racist. Pupils may look up to their teachers as being role models. If some pupils see teachers as being racist, they may also become like their teachers and be racist too. This labelling and racism can affect a child's ability to achieve as they are being knocked harshly by aspects of their identity that they were born with and cannot change. D Gilborn found that when teachers are told of what they've been doing, they are shocked because labelling and stereotyping is a subconscious thing that we do.

④ Keddie showed that labelling can affect teacher behaviour in the classroom. Teachers tend to pick Asian girls or white boys when questions are being asked in the classroom. This shows favouritism and teacher expectations. The negatively labelled children will feel there is little point in attempting to succeed. Labelling can be part of a whole school process as children are placed in sets, sometimes on the basis of social class. This can be positive or negative for children. If you are placed in a top set of hardworking students then a positive attitude would shine through and you would most likely achieve to the best of your ability. However, if you are placed in a low set, with a negative label, you will gain more status from having a negative attitude to school and this will lead you to underachieve.

Examiner commentary:

① Seren uses the technical language of labelling theory throughout the response and this shows confidence in AO1. Here, there is clear understanding that different groups of pupils may be labelled in either a positive or negative fashion.

② Seren refers to named writers accurately throughout the response. There appears to be a reference to self-fulfilling prophecy, but the point needs to be made more clearly. However, Seren does show she understands that labelling is an ongoing process.

③ This paragraph is sophisticated because it shows understanding that it is not just teachers who label students, but that other pupils may be involved in the process as well. In addition, teachers and pupils are not aware that they may be labelling pupils negatively. These are good points made in very few words.

④ The concluding paragraph continues with additional thought. Seren understands that labelling is not always a negative process; it acts to favour some students who will feel confident as a result of positive labelling. She also recognises that labelling is not personal, but institutional. Students are labelled if they are put into bands or sets and this influences their school performance.

Summative comments

Note that this is not a perfect answer, but that it shows evidence of all of the skills that are necessary for Seren to prove that she can meet the assessment objectives for this element of the course. This answer gained 18 marks overall, **AO1 was worth 10/12** and **AO2 was awarded 8/8**. Some points were a bit repetitive and Seren did not really consider the research evidence on the effects of social class on the labelling process. The idea of self-fulfilling prophecy was referred to, but not explained in any detail and it is an important part of the labelling process. This would achieve an **A grade**.

Q & A

> ## Discuss the extent to which cultural factors may affect attainment in school.
>
> *(40 marks)*

Tom's answer:

① Cultural factors have a huge effect on attainment. Depending on which culture and the norms and values of that culture, this will have an effect on attainment in schools.

② Asian culture is perceived positively by teachers. They see their culture as one based on hardworking norms and values; therefore they are encouraged in school and work hard to maintain the high rules of their culture. African-Caribbean culture is perceived negatively in schools. Their culture develops an anti-school culture and the pupils from this culture are likely to be in detention or expelled. They do not work hard and are perceived negatively by others. Therefore, they do not get the grades they need to achieve. Black culture is perceived negatively in schools. Whenever it is mentioned it is negative such as the slave trade. Black music, dress and culture is largely ignored in the curriculum and is of little relevance or no interests to common day Black culture. Therefore Black pupils and ethnic minority pupils will be uninterested in what is being taught and may find it difficult to attain the grades that they need.

③ The education system aims to give all children an equal opportunity to climb the social hierarchy. Everyone is taught the same subjects in the same way. But if a pupil chooses not to work hard in school, then they will not be able to gain the careers at the top of the hierarchy.

④ The working class are said to develop a defeatist attitude where they prefer to enjoy immediate benefits rather than make sacrifices for the social benefits later in life. Studies show that many working-class pupils see school as a negative thing in their lives. Their parents may be to blame when it comes to this as they fail to see the point in education, which is a view that is then passed down to their children. The children will develop an anti-school culture that they need to survive in the workplace like the lads.

⑤ Many children may come from a rough background of a culture where education is seen as pointless. These pupils will become confrontational with teachers and are likely to be sent out of class deducting from their learning time, therefore underachieving in a subject so they do not get the grades they want. The middle classes are seen as culturally superior. They may do well in school and follow a set of norms and values that see education as important. Pupils from a high culture background may have more money to succeed in school and they can be sent to a private school where they will receive a better education or follow into jobs closer to the top of society.

Examiner commentary:

① This is a weak opening as culture is not defined, nor is attainment. Nevertheless the link between cultural values and attainment is made clear.

② Ethnicity and attitudes to education are explored. Tom recognises that some cultural backgrounds are more responsive to education. He also recognises that the culture of schools may have a negative impact on some children's attainment. This adds breadth to the answer. Tom misses a chance to talk about the hidden curriculum, although he makes the point that the British education system tends to be ethnocentric.

③ Statements in this paragraph need to be examined with care! There are a variety of different types of school, so people's experiences of education are not the same.

④ This material could have been developed more carefully. The ideas in the first sentence are associated with Oscar Lewis and the New Right. Making that explicit link between an idea and the people who propose it would have made this a far better response. The same point applies to the comment about the lads; this is a reference to Willis's classic study, *Learning to Labour*, but this point is not made clear and is an opportunity missed.

⑤ Again, there is a reference to Bourdieu's concept of cultural capital, but that is not explained or even evaluated. The paragraph drifts into a commentary about wealth and not culture.

(6) Each culture has different norms and values. Ralph Linton defined culture as 'the whole way of life of a people, of its members ... the collection of values, attitudes and ideas which we transmit from one generation to the next'. Depending on a child's culture, this may have a serious effect on the child's attainment in education and on its chances in life. Norms can tell us the importance of education, and values that perceive other things as more important than education will lead to a negative attitude in school. Attainment in British schools is usually measured by achieving 5 A-Cs and some groups of children are more likely to do this than others.

(7) Marxists would say that the working class are a cheap source of labour for the bourgeoisie. As they do badly in school, they are channelled into low-status jobs and controlled. Overall, there are many different types of cultural effects in schools. In my opinion, I think all parents should teach the importance of education no matter what their view of it should be. If they did badly in school, they should not pass this down to their child. Schools should not just focus on the culture of the white Anglo-Saxon male child. Teachers should view all cultures equally and should not be judged on their culture.

(6) This paragraph should probably have been the introduction because culture is defined and the importance of cultural factors in educational attainment is made clear. This is where Tom shows he has the ability to think clearly about the topic. In addition, a theorist is named! Linton was an anthropologist, but Tom does not lose marks for this.

(7) This is a very weak ending. There is no explicit statement on the extent to which cultural factors explain educational attainment. Tom needed to say that cultural factors are very important or not important at all. He could have developed this point that other factors may be involved in school failure and then his conclusion would have related to the question. There is a nice reference to theory but it is underdeveloped and the final sentence actually makes very little sense. It's something that Tom would have picked up if he had re-read his answer carefully before handing the paper in.

Summative comments

Tom's answer gained 26 marks overall, **AO1 was worth 14/20** and **AO2 was awarded 12/20**. Tom had the potential to gain an excellent grade as many points relating ethnicity, class and even gender are made, but this is disorganised and it lacks supporting evidence. Research and theory are hinted at, but the references are not explicit or clear. Tom has written an answer that has breadth, but limited depth. If this answer had been planned and organised, he could have gained more AO2 marks despite his rather generalised and underdeveloped AO1. This would achieve a **C grade.**

Discuss the extent to which cultural factors may affect attainment in school.
(40 marks)

Seren's answer:

① Many writers have said that the most important factor affecting children's attainment in school is their cultural background. Culture refers to the norms and values that people have and in Britain, although we all share a culture that is British, some people have different norms and values from others. Functionalists say that middle-class children value education more than working-class children and Marxists say that the culture of middle-class children gives them an advantage. In addition, Britain is a multi-cultural society so there are people of different backgrounds in schools.

② The Marxist writer, Pierre Bourdieu said that some people are able to gain an advantage for their children because they possess cultural capital. Schools are middle class in their norms and values and middle-class people are able to give their children the skills and knowledge to succeed in school because they know how the system works. They send their children to the best schools and teach them at home so they will be able to do well. This means teachers will label middle-class children positively. This means that Bourdieu thinks culture is very important in educational success.

③ Functionalists believe that as long as the family is performing all of its functions properly then any child can achieve. This may be true for some children, because some children do well in school despite having bad home lives. Heidi Safia Mirza showed that African-Caribbean girls wanted to do well in school despite the schools being racist towards them. However, most African-Caribbean families are single parents where the mother is head of the family. This results in the boys lacking the male role model and then turning to a gang to gain powerful status. They will be disrespectful in school and reject education because they have their own subculture to fall back on. This is shown by Sewell.

④ Cultural deprivation is mainly formed when children do not have the background to do well in school. Children may go to school behind others and not do as well. Feinstein found that poor children fall behind before they get to school and some people think the problem is to do with bad parenting. However, this might also be due to linguistic deprivation and material deprivation. There is no proof that poor children have a worse culture despite Douglas who said that working-class parents did not go to parents' evenings enough. He can be criticised because working-class people may work longer hours or feel negative about school because of their own bad experiences.

⑤ There are cultural factors in school that may make some children underachieve. There is racism in schools, and some feminists have said that schools value boys. More recently, boys are said to fail because there are not enough male role models so they think education is feminine and fail. This shows that culture is important in how some children attain in school.

Examiner commentary:

① Seren has defined the terms of the question. It is clear what the essay is going to discuss. It also helps to refer to theory early in an essay as it sets a good tone.

② Very good opening reference to a cultural idea and a writer. Bourdieu is explained and the significance of his ideas is developed.

③ This opens with a good point, but it is underdeveloped as the paragraph goes on to discuss ethnicity and gender rather than functionalism. It ends less well as it is not entirely accurate. African-Caribbeans have high rates of single parenthood but it is not true that most are single parents. It can be easy to allow stereotypes and inaccuracy to slip into writing, but the occasional inaccuracy will not be penalised as marking is positive.

④ Seren shows that she understands the importance of evidence to support theory. She also explains why she has rejected a researcher's finding. This is a high level skill and is rewarded well.

⑤ This takes a wide definition of culture and makes a good point. It would have benefitted from evidence, however.

⑥ Bernstein referred to linguistic deprivation because he said that working-class people did not have access to the same language skills as middle-class children. This could be cultural because the culture of working-class children is different but it is also about language and the way people think. It is another reason why some children do not do well.

⑦ Writers from the New Right talked about the underclass and said some people were making a life by living on benefits so their children do not need to do well in school because they have already given up. This is called a culture of dependency because people live on the dole and they do not want to work and have no work ethic.

⑧ In conclusion, it can be seen that many writers from different viewpoints think that culture is very important in why some children do better in school than others, for example Indians and Chinese are more successful than Black children. However, there are other reasons why some groups of children fail and this may be to do with having material deprivation or linguistic deprivation as well. Some children go to private schools or have more facilities and they do better and that is to do with wealth. Cultural factors are important but they are not the whole picture of educational attainment in Britain.

⑥ It is not absolutely clear what point Seren is making about Bernstein here, but she is looking at cultural factors in the development of language, so credit can be given.

⑦ There is a reference to more recent theory which is then linked to a point about culture.

⑧ This is a competent conclusion and rounds the essay off well. Seren is referring to the question directly and making a judgement. It is not a good idea to introduce new ideas into a conclusion but Seren will not be penalised. She clearly has not had time to say all that she wants but has managed her time carefully enough to write a conclusion to her essay.

Summative comments

Seren has planned her answer carefully and has referred to evidence and research. Her conclusion refers directly to the question and she makes an explicit judgement on the importance of cultural factors in school attainment. Seren's answer gained **40 marks overall**. Her essay is not perfect but it hits the assessment objectives because it refers to writers, research and theory. Every single paragraph is linked to the question and there is plentiful use of evaluative language. This would achieve an **A grade.**

Mass Media

Q & A

> Outline and explain how the media creates moral panics.
> *(20 marks)*

Tom's answer:

① The media can create moral panics for many different reasons.

② Firstly, it may be a slow news day, so reporters and journalists create problems out of nothing. This was shown by Stan Cohen's account of Easter bank holiday of 1964, when there was a very slow news day. There were reports that on Brighton beach there would be huge fights between the two youth groups, the mods and rockers.

③ Cohen described the process of building up a news story as deviancy amplification. This is when the media amplifies small issues and creates bigger ones. When media amplification has taken place, like it did between mods and rockers, it can lead to the self-fulfilling prophecy. This means that by the media predicting something will happen, they then help bring it about.

④ Secondly, the media may create moral panics unnecessarily in order to divert people's attention away from other issues that are taking place. For example, Hall et al. studied how black people were labelled as muggers which created a moral panic around Britain in the 1970s. The black people were used as scapegoats in order to divert attention away from the problems which were happening within society, described as a crisis of capitalism.

⑤ The media may also create moral panics because they may have already spent a lot of money covering an issue. Journalists may feel that if they create a moral panic then they can go back to the issue that they spent a lot of money on. For example, the media created a moral panic around child abduction, so they can go back to the Madeleine McCann case. The media spent so much money reporting this case they need to keep reporting it.

⑥ Finally, the media may create moral panics in order to implement social control in society. For example, the media may introduce the moral panic of teenage pregnancy in order to make girls become more socially controlled as parents will be worried about their daughters getting caught up in the moral panic of teenage pregnancy. This, therefore, accepts the theory of Carol Smart and Frank Ferudi as they both say that girls are more socially controlled than boys by their parents because of moral panics created by the media.

Examiner commentary:

① This is a weak introduction for Tom as introductions should be longer than one line. Candidates should show the examiner that they have a good understanding of the question. Furthermore Tom makes no attempt to define what moral panics are.

② Tom begins this paragraph well by linking moral panics to slow news days and brings in Cohen's classic study of mods and rockers, although the confrontation initially took place in Clacton rather than Brighton.

③ Tom brings in some good sociological analysis in this paragraph linking moral panics to the concept of deviancy amplification. He goes on to make the point that moral panics can lead to prediction of more trouble and a self-fulfilling prophecy.

④ Tom discusses a second example of a moral panic in this paragraph in reasonable detail: Hall et al.'s study of mugging is discussed well in terms of diverting attention from a perceived crisis of capitalism.

⑤ It is important to recognise that moral panics are about deviant groups not issues. This paragraph loses focus a little but raises the example of moral panic surrounding child abductors.

⑥ This final paragraph loses a little focus whereas the concluding paragraph should respond explicitly back to the question. However, Tom links back at the end to the idea of moral panics created by the media. He deserves credit for bringing in the ideas of Smart and Ferudi here, although the connection to moral panics is limited.

Summative comments

Tom's answer scores 13 marks overall, **AO1 was worth 9/12** and **AO2 was awarded 4/8**. Tom produced a good answer here but it had weaknesses, not least the limited amount of AO2 content. Whilst he demonstrated quite good knowledge and understanding of moral panics to score well on AO1 marks, there was limited explanation and critical analysis of how the media create moral panics thus limiting the AO2 marks it could gain. This would achieve a **C grade**.

Seren's answer:

① The term moral panic was coined by Stan Cohen following the exaggerated media coverage of 'mods and 'rockers' in the 1960s. The term refers to media reactions to groups whose behaviour is regarded as threatening to societal values. Moral panics reflect an important aspect of news production in the media, which defines certain groups and activities as deviant or problematic and campaigns for a response from the authorities.

② Cohen's work focused on the media's reaction to youth 'disturbances' on Easter 1964 in Clacton, Essex. He showed how the media blew small-scale scuffles between mods and rockers out of all proportion by using headlines such as 'Day of Terror' and 'Town under siege'. This shows that not only that the events were over-reported but that newspaper coverage outweighed their importance. Moral panics are therefore a classic example of deviancy amplification where the media overreacts and sensationalises stories whilst demonising deviant groups.

③ Cohen identified three significant processes that occur within a moral panic: 'symbolisation', 'exaggeration' and 'prediction'. This means that deviant groups are turned into 'folk-devils' whose behaviour is associated with irresponsibility, lack of respect and moral degeneracy. However, it is through the process of deviancy amplification, the media encourage and increase the very behaviour they were condemning. For example, Sarah Thornton studied the moral panic that erupted over 'rave parties' in the 1990s. She found that the media panic about drug-taking simply added to its attraction for young people.

④ Both Cohen and Furedi believe that moral panics are more likely to occur in times of rapid social change. This shows when times are less stable, people are looking for scapegoats upon which to blame their insecurity. Another factor is by focusing on so-called 'problem groups' media journalists assume that like-minded 'decent' people share their moral concerns about the direction society is taking. However, Marxist sociologists think moral panics are simply a means used by editors and journalists to sell newspapers. As such it represents a good example of how the audience is manipulated by the media in order to make profits.

⑤ In conclusion, it can be seen that moral panics reflects the power of the media in defining what counts as normal and deviant behaviour. Moral panics also illustrate the effects such media labelling have on certain groups. However, McRobbie and Thornton argue that moral panics are less frequent and harder to sustain these days, as groups labelled as 'folk devils' by the media can now more effectively fight back through pressure groups and new social movements.

Examiner commentary:

① Seren has produced a good start to this answer with this introduction. Moral panics are clearly defined in relation to groups of people and linked back to news production.

② This is a strong paragraph because it looks at Cohen's study in some detail. Seren also brings in AO2 content, explaining moral panics and making a connection to the process of deviancy amplification.

③ Seren shows good knowledge of Cohen's work, by linking moral panics to symbolisation, exaggeration and prediction. She discusses moral panics in relation to Cohen's labelling deviant groups as folk devils. The paragraph goes on to make clear evaluative points; thus gaining further AO2 marks. There is useful inclusion of another study of a moral panic discussed in Thornton's research of rave parties.

④ Seren takes her answer to a sophisticated level by showing how both Cohen and Ferudi made a connection between moral panics and wider social change in society. In addition, she highlights how journalists focus upon problem groups in the construction of moral panics. She makes a good evaluative point about Marxist view of media manipulation of moral panics.

⑤ Seren rounds up this answer with a conclusion that is explicitly focused back to the question about the role of the media in constructing moral panics. She continues to include good evaluative points, this time centred around the ideas of McRobbie and Thornton.

Summative comments

Seren's answer is strong and gained 18/20 marks overall, **AO1 was worth 10/12** and **AO2 was awarded 8/8**. Its strength is that as well as demonstrating knowledge and understanding it also has an abundance of AO2 content. In terms of the mark scheme most ideas are developed so that the answer has depth and breadth and there is reference to writers and theory. She makes reference to several sociological research studies and brings in sociological theoretical analysis with her points about Marxism. Whilst Seren could have written a little more on how the media create moral panics, with contemporary examples, the answer is detailed, coherent and well structured. This would achieve an **A grade**.

Discuss the extent to which the media promotes gender stereotypes.

(40 marks)

Tom's answer:

① The media promotes gender stereotypes. This would be the view of the Marxist-feminists. Marxist-feminists say that women are still oppressed by men, so society is still very patriarchal. This would mean that women still conform to gender stereotypes such as the female being seen as the victim and the male seen as the aggressor.

② This is exemplified in Tuchman's 1978 study. Tuchman said that women are being marginalised in society and are portrayed within the media through a limited range of roles such as within the domestic area or as sex objects. Men have access to more roles in society and this is reflected in their portrayal by the media.

③ The view that the media promotes gender stereotypes could also be the view held by the neo-Marxists. The neo-Marxists believe that women prepare men for work in society, without the woman the men would not be able to work properly. Also the media creates gender stereotypes in order to make a profit, such as portraying them as sex objects in order to sell newspapers, magazines, etc. An example of this is 'page three' modelling. In today's society sex sells, so the media creates stereotypes in order to get their money.

④ The liberal feminists put less emphasis upon the view that the media creates gender stereotype, arguing that times have changed and that the media portrays women more broadly now. They argue that women are given the same opportunities as men in society and the media reflects this. For example, the television programme The Apprentice has both males and females competing for the same high profile job.

⑤ However, the media does promote gender stereotypes for both males and females. Men are also under pressure from the media to conform to their gender stereotypes of dominant, assertive males who are successful breadwinners. Connell described this stereotype as hegemonic masculinity, whereby the media implies all men are strong, intelligent and rugged and that it is not socially acceptable to be anything different.

Examiner commentary:

① Tom's introduction is quite poor in quality as it lacks focus with the question. Gender stereotypes are not clearly explained or defined and not discussed in the context of the media. The example of women as victims is not linked to media construction. There is also an assumption made within this introduction that the question is about women, whereas gender applies to both sexes. It seems that Tom has rushed into writing this answer without carefully thinking and planning its content. Had he done so, he could then have shown the examiner a good understanding of the question through the careful construction of his first paragraph.

② There are some useful points made in this paragraph by Tom. He brings in the work of Tuchman and briefly discusses her contribution to the debate on media stereotypes. Tom seems to imply that women are portrayed in only two roles (domestic and sex objects) which is a little narrow and reflects blinkered thinking. Good to include for the first time discussion about men and how the media portrays them in wider roles but this point is undeveloped and would benefit from examples.

③ Tom brings in neo-Marxist ideas here but the connection to the media is obscure as the point he makes is more relevant to the family and work. He returns to the media construction of women as sex objects stereotype and gives the example of page three. A useful inclusion in this paragraph would have been the increasing portrayal of men as sex objects by the media.

④ Tom brings in the liberal feminist perspective here to portray the view that the media has changed along with society and that women are portrayed by the media more broadly. The example of The Apprentice is given. Men are excluded from the discussion other than the point that women are portrayed by the media competing more with them.

⑤ This paragraph contains some good content. It is focused on media portrayal of male stereotypes and brings in Connell's idea of hegemonic masculinity. However, it portrays the media as presenting men in a very narrow way. Whilst there is some truth in this stereotype, postmodernist ideas could have been used to contrast this, seeing the media as more open and diverse in its portrayal of men and women.

(6) However, over time this view of Bob Connell's hegemonic masculinity has changed. As Frank Mort says, the media partly reflects and partly shapes the fact that men have also become more feminised with a huge range of beauty and cosmetic products specifically designed for men. The media thus reflects the fact that narrow stereotypes of gender are no longer relevant, as men and women are each portrayed in increasingly differentiated ways with greater similarity between them. Postmodernists refer to this process as gender convergence.

(7) In today's postmodern society, gender and gender stereotypes are less important with style becoming more important than conforming to old out-dated stereotypes. As shown in Sarah Thornton's study on Manchester club culture. Thornton found that class, gender and ethnicity boundaries have blurred and converged together. And things such as gender stereotypes are not necessary any more in today's postmodern society.

(6) Tom introduces a more evaluative tone into this paragraph. He uses Mort to compare and contrast to Connell and makes several good points about gender differentiation on the one hand and gender convergence on the other.

(7) Tom's concluding paragraph needs to have more of a focus back to the question. Good to bring in Postmodernism into this answer but it is a pity this is not discussed earlier. It is considered not good practice to bring new material into a conclusion. In addition, Thornton's study is discussed but the connection to the media is not clear.

Summative comments

Tom's answer gained 25 marks overall, **AO1 was worth 15/20** and **AO2 was awarded 10/20**. It contained good content in places and included several sociological studies; however, it never fully engaged with how the media reinforced gender stereotypes. It does recognise changes to society and hence media representations and does discuss representations of men as well as women. AO2 content needed to be more explicit throughout the answer. This would achieve a **C grade**.

Discuss the extent to which the media promotes gender stereotypes.

(40 marks)

Seren's answer:

① Gender stereotypes and inequality have been represented and reinforced by the media significantly and because of this, Marxist-feminists such as Benston have explained that women are seen as profit-making for the media industry. Women are portrayed as housewives, as mothers and as sex objects by the media. She explained that lots of adverts use women as sex objects as a means of selling products. On the other hand, liberal-feminists such as Greer explained that the representation of women is becoming better and they are no longer just seen as housewives or in domestic situations. Radical feminists argue that the mass media portrays women as someone who needs to take care of men and as people who need patriarchal control. They also argue that women are portrayed in a narrow way, such as in traditional jobs and roles for a woman.

② Marxist-feminist and radical feminist views are both highly negative about media representations. They both see the media as an agent of social control for women and to some extent men. Women are shown in the media how they should present themselves and how they should be in order to be a good wife. Men are still primarily portrayed as breadwinners and providers, someone women can be dependent upon. Because of this, the media can be viewed as promoting and reinforcing gender stereotypes.

③ Naomi Wolf explained that women are only represented in the media as people who need to be attractive – the 'beauty myth'. She explained that the media shows stereotypical views of women. For example, the stereotype of an attractive woman is slim, blonde and a sex object who can cook and take care of their husbands and give them comfort. She explains that different roles and types of women are not shown. Therefore the view that people would gain of women is very narrow. Also she explained that most films are shown in a way that is aimed at men rather than both genders.

④ Tuchman would also support the views of Marxist and radical feminists by explaining that the media shows women in low-status jobs and it shows that women have limited roles in society. For example, they are shown in the media as mothers, sex objects and if they are shown in any other way than this, the media will portray them negatively. For example, they would show women getting divorced for not being able to be a good mother or wife.

Examiner commentary:

① Seren starts her answer confidently and compares three types of feminism and their views on the media's role in stereotyping women. She could have flagged up alternative perspectives such as Postmodernism here. It is a pity she does not explain what stereotypes are. Like Tom above, she implies by her content in this introduction that this answer on gender stereotypes is about women and excludes men.

② Although this paragraph is mainly about women, there is recognition of the media acting as a controlling force on men, too, and men are discussed as breadwinners/providers. Good to make the last sentence focused on the question.

③ Seren brings in the work of Wolf and discusses this effectively in terms of media stereotypes. It is a pity that this answer has limited focus on media stereotyping of men so far.

④ Whilst Seren deserves credit for bringing in the work of Tuchman here, there is repetition of earlier points. However, the idea that when women are portrayed outside the typical stereotypes, they are shown to have negative consequences is a good point to make. The example Seren gives is appropriate and good.

(5) However, Gautlett explains that the media have become better in representing women in films, advertising and music videos. Gautlett explains that only 3% of women in the media are shown as housewives and the rest are shown as women earning money, often in high status jobs. She also points out that the voices of advertisers are more likely to be women.

(6) Postmodernists would explain that the media is now an industry which tells both men and women how they should make themselves sexy and both men and women are represented as sex objects. However, they recognise how the media reflects an increasingly diverse and fragmented society. Therefore the media no longer has a role of telling us what we should be or how we should wear our clothes. Therefore, according to the postmodernist view, both males and females are no longer represented according to rigid stereotypes. For example, not all men are working in traditional jobs such as the male nurses who are leading characters in Casualty, and women increasingly portrayed in high status jobs.

(7) In conclusion the media does promote gender stereotypes to some extent and both men and women appear to be influenced by these stereotypes. However, as society becomes more gender equal and diverse, so the media reflects this in its representations of both men and women which is undermining the narrowness of gender stereotypes.

(5) This is another generally well-written and constructed paragraph that recognises change in media representations and hence stereotypes.

(6) This is a strong paragraph where Seren introduces postmodernist ideas and how these differ to the feminist views portrayed so far. Discussion is divided between men and women, bringing more of a gender balance into the answer.

(7) Seren concludes her answer with a short and crisp final paragraph that is focussed on the question. She recognises change within society and the media and the argument that whilst stereotypes remain, they are in the eyes of some, becoming weaker.

Summative comments

Seren has produced a detailed answer here to the question, but it is not perfect. There is an imbalance in the answer, with female stereotypes discussed far more than male stereotypes in the media. However, even though the bulk of the answer is about women, it is well constructed into an answer with good coherence. Because most ideas are developed so that the answer has depth as well as some breadth and there is reference to writers and theory, Seren gained 34/40 marks for this answer with **17/20 for AO1** and **17/20 for AO2**. This would achieve an **A grade**.

Quickfire Answers

SY1
The Compulsory Core

① Sociologists are interested in culture because culture is the basis of human society.

② Children who have not been socialised by humans are not able to behave as humans behave. They cannot fit in to society. Puppy boy Horst is an example of a feral child that proves how important socialisation is to humans.

③ What we learn is ways of behaving and thinking. How we learn involves the mechanisms involved in acquiring what we know.

④ Formal control involves written rules and punishments whereas informal control does not. Social control is very similar to socialisation but is more involved with sanctions whereas socialisation also includes imitation of role models.

⑤ Subliminal messages are messages that we are unaware of, so we might be learning something without realising it.

⑥ Informal sanctions are used such as shunning and making a person feeling guilty for their behaviour by ignoring them.

Families and Culture

① It is difficult to decide on a simple definition of the term family because there are so many different family types. One definition would mean that many family types would not be regarded as families.

② Reconstituted families have become more common because of divorce and also because people still value marriage and family life.

③ The ideology of family means a particular way of thinking about family. It usually refers to the functionalist belief that the nuclear family is the best type of family. This is sometimes referred to as familism.

④ The New Right are supporters of marriage, so divorce is seen as a threat to family life. There is disagreement about this view and it should be debated with supporting evidence.

⑤ Sociologists are interested in demographic change, as it can be an indicator of changing attitudes or it might herald further social change.

⑥ An aging population can put pressure on welfare and health care services. It can also have an impact on caring and on family structures and relationships.

⑦ Functionalists present a one-sided view suggesting that the family always performs positive functions.

⑧ Marxists only focus on capitalism and the negative aspects of the family.

⑨ Feminists claim that family life exploits women and there is compelling evidence to suggest that this might be the case for some women.

⑩ Abuse and exploitation inside is evidence that some families are far from the safe haven of comfort and security suggested in the warm bath analogy.

⑪ There is some evidence that younger couples and same sex couples are more egalitarian and that men are getting more involved in child care. However, most evidence suggests that conjugal relationships are unequal.

⑫ Increased life expectancy puts greater pressure on the NHS and on Social Security benefits. It changes the balance of working and non-working population. But it also means that life can be rich and rewarding for older people, and closer relationships between grandparents and grandchildren are more common.

Youth Culture

① Young people had money to spend on themselves after the Second World War ended. There was more leisure time because people started to work shorter hours. There was increased access to consumer goods such as fashion and cinema.

② • Only young people can be part of youth cultures.
• Youth cultures often have special fashions, styles and music.
• Youth cultures are often deviant in some way.
• Some youth cultures are deliberately rejecting of mainstream culture and often provocative in some way, by being rebellious or different.

③ Obviously, only you can answer this question from your own experiences, as youth cultures tend to shift and change very quickly. Some youth cultures are very localised whereas spectacular youth cultures were often global in scope.

④ • Functionalists say it is a rite of passage.
• Marxists say it is a resistance to authority and capitalism.
• Interactionists say that it is a way of creating a personal identity for oneself.
• Postmodernists say that people buy into youth cultures and that they are created as a way of encouraging young people to consume media products.

⑤ *Functionalist*
Strength – sees youth culture as normal and not a problem, so is sympathetic to young people.

Weakness – ignores the fact that not all young people join up to youth culture.

Marxist
Strength – explains why some youth cultures are deviant.

Weakness – romanticises youth cultures in the way that it wants to see young people as rebelling against capitalism. This means it ignores the way that some youth cultures are consumerist.

Interactionist
Strength – explains how some youth cultures become deviant.

Weakness – ignores social structures and does not explain why people become deviant in the first place.

Postmodernist
Strength – explains why there is a wide range of different youth styles available to choose from.

Weakness – this theory is not easily testable and the evidence therefore is not strong.

⑥ • Some male youth groups have challenged traditional gender patterns in order to shock or to criticise society in some way.
• Middle-class boys have been happier to challenge traditional gender patterns than working-class boys.
• Girls have often challenged male patterns of behaviour to assert themselves.
• Other groups have reinforced gender patterns as a backlash against feminism and as a way of asserting masculinity.

⑦ *Differences*
- Male youth cultures have tended to be more public and girls more private.
- Female youth cultures have not been described, whereas there is a long literature on male youth culture.
- Very young women tend to form very intense one-to-one relationships, whereas boys are more likely to form gangs.

Similarities
- Young women form gangs later in youth, and there have been criminal girl gangs.
- Many young women subscribe to lad culture and have become ladettes.

⑧ Some youth cultures have been heavily associated with class. The early youth cultures were mainly working class. More recently, postmodernists argue that class is not an important dynamic. This can be challenged because Hoodie and Chav culture is working class in style.

⑨ Some youth cultures have been very accepting of ethnic minorities and have even adopted their music and styles. Other youth cultures have been very racist and antagonistic towards members of cultural minorities.

⑩
- Spectacular youth cultures existed before the 1980s, but neotribes are recent in origin.
- Spectacular youth cultures seemed to be about substance rather than style, so they had alternative values; neotribes are about style rather than shared values.
- Neotribes are consumerist rather than cultural.

⑪ 1. Small incident exaggerated by the media.
2. Description of the deviant behaviours.
3. Public expressions of moral outrage.
4. Growth of behaviour, as more young people are attracted to the behaviour.
5. Further exaggerated news stories and over-reaction by authority.

⑫
- The nature of work has changed and it is less easy to get a job.
- Traditional patterns of gender have changed.
- Qualifications are more necessary for success.
- Social norms and values regarding sex and sexuality have changed.
- There are more consumer goods.

- The nature and style of media and media content are different.
- Young people are less involved in political parties and more involved in single political issues.
- Many young people are likely to be in debt and therefore less able to leave home in early adulthood.

⑬ *For*
- They adopt clothing styles that may offend older people.
- Most are associated with leisure drugs of some kind.
- They adopt styles that are particular and unusual.
- Many are criminal or semi-criminal.

Against
- Many youth cultures are simply a style choice rather than a lifestyle choice.
- Many people, not just young people, abuse leisure drugs.
- Youth styles quickly become mainstream fashion for older people.
- Sometimes the criminality is over-stated to shock.

SY2
Research Methods

① Sociology is a social science and therefore has to go beyond common-sense thinking by coming up with ideas based upon quantitative and qualitative evidence derived from a systematic research process. Sociologists have to be able to defend their findings based on their research evidence.

② Reliable means that if the research were repeated, the same results would be obtained. This shows that the findings are sound and not just accidental or coincidental. Data that is reliable gives a piece of research credibility and therefore the likelihood that it will be taken seriously.

③ Researchers have a duty of care towards the people they are researching. Asking questions about sensitive subjects such as anorexia or personal attack could bring back memories that people had thought they had dealt with. This could lead to anxiety, depression or even thoughts of suicide.

④ Gagging contracts enable the government to control what researchers can publish. They can potentially limit the release of negative or embarrassing findings, although this goes against the spirit of open government.

⑤ The main reason is when samples are small; they therefore cannot reflect the full characteristics of the target population.

⑥ Postal (or web-based) questionnaires are good for accessing people dispersed over a wide geographical area or a group who are isolated from the researcher. The key disadvantage of this method is a low response rate.

⑦ Compared to structured interviews, these allow respondents to develop and elaborate their answers and therefore encourage the collection of qualitative data that is higher in validity.

⑧ This term means when participant observers become so close to the people they are observing that they become one of them and as a consequence their objective judgement can become clouded.

⑨ Because such sources were compiled by other researchers, often it is not known exactly how the data was collected. Assumptions have to be made that the data was collected in a systematic and rigorous manner, but sometimes this cannot be verified.

⑩ Official statistics already exist, so they save researchers time and money as they are often freely available. On the whole they are accurate and provide data on large samples, such as birth, death and marriage rates. Whilst official crime rates grossly underestimate the true level of crime, they still give an indication of patterns and trends. Official statistics are often produced annually, or even monthly, so tend to be up-to-date.

Education

① We need to educate children into the basic skills needed in our society. The education system is an important agency of socialisation and social control. Children can be trained to take their future roles in society.

② 1960s – Change to comprehensive schools.

1980s – Schools governed by market forces and encouraged to be in competition.

1990s – Introduction of National Curriculum, new forms of school such as City Technology colleges.

2000s – Return to traditional educational patterns such as selection for places, changes to the education system and more target setting for teachers.

③ Governments pass regular legislation concerned with education for political reasons, so they can win votes from parents. They also do it for ideological reasons because they have beliefs about the nature of education. Governments have also been concerned to control their spending, and education is a major expense for the country, at over 4% of all government expenditure.

④ *Advantages*
- If schools are in competition, they have incentives to improve.
- Parents can choose the most appropriate schools for their children.

Disadvantages
- The differences between the best schools and the worst schools may be exaggerated as middle-class parents opt away from poorly performing schools.
- Children who are unlikely to gain the necessary grades will be rejected by the best schools.

⑤ *Similarities*
- They look at the whole of the education system rather than the individuals who work or learn in it.
- They see the education system as a system of social control and social organisation.

Differences
- Functionalists view the education system as a positive and useful system. Conflict theories see it as a form of ideological control.
- Functionalists claim that everyone has an equal chance of success depending on ability. Conflict theories blame the education system for oppressing some groups.

⑥ • Structural theories take an overview of the whole education system; labelling theory looks at processes within schools.
- Structural theories account for social reasons for inequality; labelling theories look at the effects of inequality.

⑦ There is a direct link between qualifications and subsequent life chances such as pay, health and opportunity. The higher the qualifications that a person has, the easier life is likely to be.

⑧ • Middle-class people are more likely to have access to the cultural capital that can benefit their children in the education system.

- Middle-class people are more likely to be supportive of schools and to be able to speak to teachers with confidence, so they have strategies to support their children.
- Middle-class people are more likely to support their children through expenditure on educational equipment.
- Middle-class people are more likely to speak in the same way as teachers, using the same words and style of speaking.

⑨ • More likely to experience ill-health and poor nourishment.
- More likely to have parental problems related to the stress of poverty.
- More likely to experience parental relationship breakdown.
- Schools are likely to reject children from poorer areas.
- Poor children have less access to school trips and school outings.
- Poor children have lower attendance.
- Poorer children may be embarrassed by free school meals.

⑩ • Labelling of certain pupils.
- Setting, streaming and banding on the basis of behaviour rather than ability.
- Teacher attitudes and behaviours.
- The effectiveness of teaching and management systems.
- Gender discrimination against girls.
- Inability to support the needs of boys.
- Institutional racism and ethnocentricity.
- The nature and locality of the schools themselves.

⑪ *Yes*
- Most teach to the National Curriculum.
- They are inspected by Ofsted in England and Estyn in Wales and expected to reach a similar standard.

No
- There are differences in funding between schools.
- There is a private education system.
- Schools have different catchment areas with different classes of children.
- Some schools have high percentages of difficult children with special needs.

Mass Media

① • Concentration of ownership.
- Domination of (usually US-based) multinational corporations.
- Electronic colonialism (McPhail).
- Cultural penetration of Western values into developing countries.

② Because pluralists see the media as an important promoter of democracy, since for most people it is their main source of political information. Media barons, according to pluralists, promote a cross-section of views that broadly reflect and reinforce consensus norms and values.

③ Churnalism is a term coined by Nick Davies and refers to the over-reliance by journalists on press releases by government and other organisations which they then rewrite as journalism. This is partly to save money by avoiding expensive investigations and partly through laziness of modern journalists who rely on second-hand stories.

④ The news media like to sensational stories as well as demonising deviant groups. Cohen wrote about how moral panics are an example of deviancy amplification whereby the media exaggerate the deviance of the folk devils in order to sell newspapers and enhance television audiences.

⑤ The Frankfurt School comprised mainly refugees who had fled Nazi Germany to the USA. They had seen first hand the expert use the Nazis made of media propaganda and its influence on the people. This led them to develop the hypodermic syringe model highlighting the powerful effect of the media.

⑥ The new media refers to digital technology, particularly that which offers convergence in the form of offering several media on one platform, such as 3G mobile phones that offer media such as the Internet through which social networking, radio and television can be accessed.

⑦ This is a negative term, used especially by conflict sociologists, to refer to the way multinational companies exert cultural imperialism and electronic colonialism on developing countries (as discussed in the first page of the section on mass media).

⑧ He argues that not only does the media reflect the diversity of gender representation in a postmodern society but also helps to shape them by representing women and men in a wide range of roles.

⑨ They are often presented as 'other' groups, implying that they are not part of mainstream society. In addition, they can become demonised groups such as the labelling of young black males as muggers (Hall *et al.*) or the Islamophobia of linking Muslims generally with international terrorism.

⑩ Most journalists are middle class and were educated at private school. Hegemonic (neo-Marxist) theorists argue that their background shapes the generally conservative values of the media.